Understanding Sunday School

LEADERS
AND
TEACHERS
BUILDING
TOGETHER

EVANGELICAL TEACHER TRAINING ASSOCIATION
110 Bridge Street · Box 327
Wheaton, Illinois 60189

Courses in the Preliminary Certificate Program
  Old Testament Survey—Law and History
  Old Testment Survey—Poetry and Prophecy
  New Testament Survey
  Understanding People
  Understanding Teaching or Teaching Techniques
  Understanding Sunday School

ISBN 0-910566-06-2

First Edition
3 4 5 6 7 8 / 5 4 3 2 1 0 9 8 7 6 5

Library of Congress catalog card number: 81-67935
© 1981 by Evangelical Teacher Training Association
Printed in U.S.A.

CONTENTS

Introduction

The basic educational ministry of the church is the Sunday school. This is true whether the church has a multifaceted educational program or concentrates its educational ministry in weekly Sunday school classes.

Understanding Sunday School endeavors to clarify the purposes, organization, and ministries of the Sunday school for all related to and serving in it. It will be profitable reading and study for leaders, teachers, and students; for all share in its benefits and outreach.

At the end of each chapter in this text are guide questions for study and discussion. There are also suggested activities to aid the student in applying the truths presented. Careful and consistent use of these portions of the text will enable the student to better relate the course material to practical Christian ministry.

An instructor's guide has been prepared to assist those who teach the course as part of E.T.T.A.'s leadership training program. The guide includes easy-to-follow lesson plans and other suggestions for class presentation. To further enrich the course, masters for preparing overhead transparencies have been developed to add interest and appeal to class sessions. A cassette with a brief workbook is also available for use in classroom presentations or for individual enrichment.

Understanding Sunday School relates the Sunday school to today's church and current witness. This book should be studied by everyone who is or desires to be involved in its ministry.

The Challenge of
Sunday School

1

The pressures of our times make Sunday school an imperative. Its function and purpose come from the Word of God. Deuteronomy 31:12-13 describes God's plan, "Gather the people together, men and women and children, and thy stranger that is within thy gates, that they may hear, and that they may learn, and fear the Lord your God, and observe to do all the words of this law; And that their children, which have not known any thing, may hear, and learn to fear the Lord your God."

In the New Testament the commands to teach are no less direct. The words of Jesus serve as an example: "Go therefore and make disciples of all the nations, . . . teaching them to observe all things whatever I have commanded you" (Matt. 28:19, 20 NKJV).

Today, against a background of terrorism, crime, and the threat of world conflict, the Sunday school must continue to disseminate the basic truths found in Scripture and bring people to a true understanding of the gospel.

Churches may change the name of Sunday school to something with a more contemporary sound, they may develop programs which vary from the traditional structure, but the essential teaching thrust goes on. The course, *Understanding Sunday School*, is concerned with emphasizing the continuing and even increasing necessity for the strategic teaching programs which are carried out in the Sunday school.

DEVELOPMENT OF THE SUNDAY SCHOOL

The past always makes a contribution to the present. Such is the case with the Sunday school. The efforts and sacrifices of those who have gone before to make the Sunday school a major element for Christian teachings cannot go unnoticed.

BEGINNINGS IN ENGLAND

Though his early efforts were basically trial and error, Robert Raikes, a British publisher, sought to meet the needs of the vast number of poor children in Gloucester by establishing a Sunday education program. His Sunday school was conducted in the kitchen of Mrs. Meredith in Sooty Alley, the worst slum of that area. The objectives were to keep children off the streets, teach them to read and write, and bring them into contact with the gospel. The only requirements were that the children had clean hands, clean faces, and combed hair. Religious instruction came as they were taken to church in the afternoon, much to the dismay of the congregation where they attended. Though Raikes' efforts met opposition, they contributed to a growing movement which led to a worldwide ministry.

SUNDAY SCHOOL IN AMERICA

The beginning of the Sunday school in the United States was similar to that in England as William Elliott opened his kitchen to children of Oak Ridge, Virginia, for teaching on Sunday. His efforts were encouraged by various individuals and finally the church began to see the possibilities. This period of experimentation led to establishing city Sunday school unions in Boston, New York, and Philadelphia. The objectives of the unions were to encourage teaching at the level of the child, to emphasize the value of children and youth, to promote teaching aids, and to improve classroom instruction.

THE ORGANIZED SUNDAY SCHOOL

In 1817 the American Sunday School Union (now American Missionary Fellowship) was formed to promote lesson materials, furnish selected outlines and teaching aids, and send forth its missionaries to establish rural or branch Sunday schools throughout pioneer America. This soon led to the first National Convention in 1832 by which time the ASSU had already established 2,867 schools. So rapidly did the popularity of the Sunday school movement spread that it became an international movement with the World Sunday School Convention convening in London in 1889. In a century, the meager beginnings in Sooty Alley had spread throughout the world.

In the early decades of the twentieth century, however, the American Sunday school movement steadily declined. Evangelicals became concerned and, under the initial interest of members of the National Association of Evangelicals, the National Sunday

School Association organized in 1945. As a result of its conventions and assistance, many regional and local associations for Sunday school improvement were formed, most of which are still active and vibrant organizations.

CURRICULUM DEVELOPMENT

Sunday schools in the early years had no standard curriculum. Most of them followed the European catechetical methods stressing memory work and rote learning. The emphasis was always on the Bible but teachers were given a wide choice of content, memory passages, and classroom techniques. In 1824 the New York Sunday School Union began to produce "selected lessons" and the American Sunday School Union published the "Union Questions." This offered some uniformity but was not widespread enough to allay the forthcoming confusion of materials. John H. Vincent and B.F. Jacobs encouraged uniformity at the ASSU convention, which ultimately led to formulating the International Lesson Committee in 1872. This committee still functions to design the International Uniform Lesson Series consisting of the title, designated Scriptures, and the "golden text" for a seven-year period. Departmentalized lessons by independent and denominational publishers followed and were widely accepted.

FUNCTIONS OF THE SUNDAY SCHOOL

Sunday school is of immeasurable value to the church. Although for decades it was fashionable to describe the Sunday school as the "teaching arm" or the "evangelism arm" of the church, today Christian educators do not view any church ministry as an appendage or a part. Sunday school may emphasize the teaching role just as a missionary conference emphasizes the task of world evangelization, but both are parts of a whole. A fragmented concept of the church is contrary to the biblical picture in Ephesians 4:1-6. However, the Sunday school does fulfill several distinctive functions in its educational role.

REACHING PEOPLE

One of the primary objectives of the church should be reaching people. Visitors who attend church services, people in the community who have no church affiliation and/or little training in the Word of God, and parents of Sunday school children all represent a rich harvest of outreach and missionary endeavor. A well-planned and carefully-executed program of visitation governs the success of growth. This will necessitate continued training of the entire educational staff.

A concern for reaching people does not automatically develop in a Sunday school, it is caught from its leadership. If the director of education, board of Christian education, Sunday school superintendent, and departmental superintendents are genuinely committed to an outreach ministry, Sunday school evangelism will be effective.

Visitation is a vital step in actually reaching people. A Sunday school may have adequate space properly arranged, a sufficient number of classes, excellent teaching methods, meaningful worship sessions, but without visitation all these will be short of complete success. The Scriptures give ample indication of a basis and motive for visitation. The benefits of visitation are sure and certain, but only correct methods of visitation will get the job adequately done. This involves the leadership setting the example, making assignments, and training workers to do an effective job.

TEACHING PEOPLE

The main thrust of the Sunday school is to teach the Bible so that people may be brought into a personal relationship with the Lord Jesus Christ.

Teaching the Word of God is the supreme motive and desire of those involved in Christian education. The entire Sunday school staff must recognize its task to implant the Word of God in the hearts and minds of individuals. Teachers have the opportunity and obligation to bring their students into a personal relationship with Christ as Savior and Lord. The fact that the Bible presents the way of life and of access into the presence of God, and that people who are not in Sunday school may never study the Bible further stresses the Sunday school's importance.

DISCIPLING PEOPLE

If Sunday school ministry is really on target, the church will see as one of its obligations the discipling of individuals into the service of Christ and his church. Christian growth means more than indoctrination in Bible knowledge. Growing in Christlikeness must include stewardship and dedication to service. A total ministry of discipling should include teaching the Word of God, development and practice of godly living, and emphasis upon the principle of service. Later chapters in this book will stress these topics.

PURPOSES OF THE SUNDAY SCHOOL

During the past quarter century, considerable study has been given to defining the purposes of Christian education at the local church level. Yet many have failed to recognize the place of the Sunday school in meeting these purposes. Leaders charged with teaching the Word of God must recognize the direction in which the total educational program of the church is moving. The following is a brief and representative list of the major objectives of the great task of Christian education in the Sunday school.

ATTAINING A PERSONAL KNOWLEDGE OF GOD

The Father

Christian education seeks to help the individual see God as sovereign, infinite, eternal, and unchanging in his being; recognize all his attributes including holiness, justice, goodness, truth, and love; and accept him as the creator and rightful owner of the universe. This aim should be properly interpreted to the various age levels so that individuals can understand God as the heavenly Father who is personally interested in the welfare of his children and who has a master plan for each life.

The Son, Jesus Christ

Christ is God. When this is recognized, Christ can rightly be seen and served as lord and master. Christ is the head of the church, and a friend and advocate who pleads the sinner's case before God the Father. His coming, death, and resurrection perfected our salvation. A personal experience with him is vital to eternal life and forgiveness of sin.

The Holy Spirit

Sunday school students must be taught that the Holy Spirit is the third person of the Trinity, possessing the attributes of God. Students should learn that the Holy Spirit convicts of sin, seals the believer with assurance of salvation, and baptizes the believer into the body of Christ. The Christian educator will teach the role of the Holy Spirit as indweller, controller, and the one who empowers every believer in Christ, revealing the deeper things of God's Word.

DEVELOPING VIBRANT CHRISTIAN LIFE

Living daily for Christ in the power of the Holy Spirit and according to the principles of the Word of God necessitates a growing spiritual life characterized by daily devotion. This requires a social life which conforms to the standards of Christian conduct represented in the Word of God. It means instruction in the Word of God which will result in seeking the Lord's will in all the important decisions throughout life.

GAINING AN UNDERSTANDING OF THE WORD OF GOD

People need to be taught that the Bible is the complete, authoritative, infallible revelation from God to man which convicts him of sin, reveals the plan of salvation producing faith in Christ, and nourishes him for spiritual growth. People need to experience the Word of God supplying truth for daily living. The Bible also offers comfort in every experience of life and ultimately increases our love for Christ, thus guiding us into his image.

OBTAINING AN APPRECIATION OF OUR CHRISTIAN HERITAGE

Christian education should include the use of Christian literature, music, and art. A confused world needs the stabilizing effect of Christians and their philosophy on cultural patterns. Perhaps a unified and articulate Christian philosophy with a biblical interpretation of life can help stem the tide of death and destruction in modern society.

ACHIEVING A LOYALTY TO THE CHURCH

Loyalty necessitates adequate instruction about the church as the body of Christ and each believer's responsibility to Christ as the head of the Church. An effective Sunday school emphasizes the local church as the hub of the Christian community and encourages participation in its ministries.

ACQUIRING A SENSE OF RESPONSIBILITY FOR OUR COMMUNITIES

Christian education seeks to help believers make Christ known through individual witness and cooperative expression on moral convictions. Christian influence should be felt in every area of human endeavor, in life as a whole—the Christian home, schools and colleges, hospitals, civic activities, employer-employee relationships.

DEVELOPING A SENSE OF RESPONSIBILITY TOWARD THE WORLD

The missionary impact of the Bible is inescapable. Therefore, Christian education seeks to lead people into a dedication of life with the obligation of yielding time, talents, wealth, and will to God. As we teach God's truth, people will be led into the service of sharing the Word of God throughout the world under the direction of the Spirit of God.

The Sunday school is a vital part of the educational role of the church. In helping fulfill the purposes of Christian education, it enlarges the church's ministry.

SUMMARY

From its humble beginnings in England and America, the Sunday school has fulfilled a vital need. Today it is the most powerful educational ministry of the church. This role of the Sunday school is carried out through reaching, teaching, and discipling.

Though many forces have worked contrary to the Sunday school, it has endured and come back strong. The Sunday school has remained true to its purposes of bringing men, women, and children to a personal knowledge of the triune God. It has persisted in stressing the need to live a vibrant Christian life based on the precepts found in the Scriptures and has encouraged the appreciation of our rich Christian heritage and our responsibility of loyalty to our church, community, and the entire world.

With principles and purposes like these is it any wonder that the Lord has blessed the Sunday school through these past two centuries? It is clearly the most effective agency we have ever had for Christian education.

TO THE STUDENT

At the end of each chapter various types of review emphases are provided. The first section contains discussion questions and application suggestions. The questions are content-centered and each is answered in the text. In reviewing each chapter, study these questions and formulate additional ones. Discussion of these may add fuller appreciation of the lesson content.

Application activities are designed to aid in applying the chapter teaching to specific situations in your own church situation.

REVIEW AND DISCUSSION QUESTIONS

1. Why is Sunday school imperative?
2. What is the role of the Sunday school?

3. Give a brief historical sketch of the development of the Sunday school.
4. What are the main purposes of the Sunday school?
5. Discuss the place of the Word of God in the Sunday school.
6. What should a program of development and enlistment include?
7. What are the major objectives of the overall church program?

APPLICATION ACTIVITIES

1. Involve the group in a scriptural search for those verses or sections of Scripture which fortify and give examples of the major objectives of the Sunday school.
2. Examine the roll of a children's Sunday school class in your church to determine the number of prospective Sunday school members that are among parents of these children.
3. Examine how visitation or contacts made by church personnel for the past three months have influenced either attendance or enrollment in the Sunday school. Project, in terms of numbers in attendance and enrollment, the ultimate results a well-planned visitation program would have on the growth of your Sunday school.
4. Examine the aim of several individual lessons in your quarterly to discover into which of the nine major objectives of Christian education each of these lessons fit.
5. Reviewing the major objectives of Christian education, reword these objectives to meet the age level and needs of the group in which you are particularly interested or with which you are presently working.

RESOURCES

Daniel, Eleanor; Wade, John; and Gresham, Charles. *Introduction to Christian Education.* Cincinnati, OH: Standard Publishing, 1980.

Towns, Elmer. *The Successful Sunday School and Teachers Guidebook.* Carol Stream, IL: Creation House, 1976.

Willis, Wesley R. *200 Years . . . And Still Counting!* Wheaton, IL: Victor Books, 1979.

Organizing For Action

2

Good organization is vital to effective Christian education. In a broad sense, Sunday school organization is a combination of the necessary individuals, equipment, facilities, materials, and tools. When all these components are assembled together in a systematic and effective way, the Sunday school may then accomplish the objectives laid before it. Each staff member needs to recognize his responsibility in the organization and the ultimate objectives which the organization is designed to meet. He will also recognize the need for cooperation with that individual or group of individuals to which he is answerable. Such a concept of organization in the Sunday school program will raise the standards and quality of leadership and will, in the eyes of the total church membership, elevate the entire teaching task.

Understanding the benefits of a well-organized Sunday school is essential to the development and implementation of a Sunday school program.

BENEFITS OF ORGANIZATION

Sometimes people confuse organization with bureaucracy. Organization, though, is more properly equated with words such as "order" and "efficiency." If we are to be effective in communicating the Word of God in the Sunday school, we must go about our task "decently and in order." There are many benefits which organization can bring to the Sunday school.

DEVELOPS TEAMWORK

In a successful sports team, each player sacrifices his own desire for personal achievement and cooperates with his teammates. Star players alone cannot win games. Each member must perform his specific part in each play. So it is in Sunday school. The united effort of all staff members produces far greater progress than the unrelated efforts of individuals.

IDENTIFIES RESPONSIBILITIES

Unorganized Sunday schools are usually ineffective. Organization makes it possible to have a clear definition of responsibility for assigned tasks and indicates who is responsible for what and to whom.

PROVIDES FOR EFFICIENT TEACHING

The Sunday school exists to teach. There are other ministries, but teaching is its first priority. The first objective of organization is the creation of the proper environment for quality teaching. Organization does not create effective teaching but it does cultivate, enhance, and facilitate it. A well-organized Sunday school provides comfortable, adequate classroom space and uninterrupted teaching time. It encourages regularity and punctuality in attendance.

CLARIFIES THE PURPOSE OF GOD'S OVERALL PROGRAM

Organization also helps define the Sunday school's functions and purposes as related to the total educational program of the church. Disciplined workers learn to organize their efforts together in love "to prepare God's people for works of service, so that the body of Christ may be built up until we all reach unity in the faith and in the knowledge of the Son of God and become mature, attaining to the whole measure of the fullness of Christ" Eph. 4:12, 13 (NIV).

FOCUSES THE AIM AND DIRECTION OF TEACHING AND LEARNING

Organization gives aim, form, and drive to building an effective curriculum. Sunday school leaders must know what they believe. They must have evangelistic fervor and spiritual depth. They know how to relate current issues to what the Bible says. The philosophy of Christian education has to be clearly distinguished from every philosophy that denounces the authority of the Word of God. Organization can help teachers and leaders know what should be taught, why it is important, and how best to present it.

ENLISTS TALENT, TRAINING, AND EXPERIENCE OF ALL MEMBERS

Some church members contribute little or nothing in worthwhile service. The church should be organized to develop servants who serve! The Sunday school is the workshop for achieving that goal.

The church needs leaders and each department in the Sunday school requires teachers and assistants. Opportunities for ministry through the Sunday school are limitless. Only an organized Sunday school can recruit, orient, and relate members to positions which best fit their talents, interests, and experience. Organization gives people opportunities to explore new fields of service which may differ from previous interest. It leads them to discover new potentials within themselves—some followers become leaders. In helping to create an individual sense of belonging, organization serves as an important means in the development of Christian character.

A church which trains its members to teach develops their spiritual lives and makes a valuable impact on its community. The well-organized Sunday school can discover leaders, disciple students, and deepen the spiritual life of the church.

ENCOURAGES COMMUNITY OUTREACH

Simply reminding members of the teaching staff and students to invite people to come to Sunday school is not going to effectively reach out into the community. But an organized program of outreach which recruits, trains, supervises, and evaluates those who are committed to community evangelism will bring new people into the fellowship. The very organized nature of the Sunday school with its emphasis on groupings and discipleship offers a solid place to start an effective outreach program.

PERSONNEL IN ORGANIZATION

Sunday school staff-line organization includes personnel organized in terms of administration, supervision, teaching, and supportive staff. Administration is basically the function of the pastor, minister or director of Christian education, Sunday school superintendent, and coordinating boards or committees. Major responsibilities of these individuals or committees should include: determining aims, establishing policies, and giving general oversight in reaching the objectives sought.

Supervision directs the operation of the organization in realizing these aims. Administration, supervision, and supporting staff exist to make possible the teacher's job: confronting people with the truths of God's Word; leading them to a personal relationship with the Lord Jesus Christ; and grounding them in their faith.

Three main spiritual gifts are helpful in Sunday school leadership.

ADMINISTRATION—I COR. 12:28

The New Testament word which is sometimes translated "administrator" literally means "helmsman" or "overseer." There is an obvious emphasis on leadership, decision-making, and general supervision of ministry in the local church. For purposes of church education, pastors, directors of education, and Sunday school superintendents are all part of administration.

EVANGELISM—EPH. 4:11

Not every Christian has the gift of evangelism but every Christian has the responsibility to witness. Because Sunday school is the principal ministry to children during their formative years and young people in their most impressionable years, every opportunity for evangelism must be seized. The claims of Christ should be presented clearly in every Sunday school concerned with following or carrying-out its biblical mandate.

EDUCATION—ROM. 12:7

The educational phase of the Sunday school is separate and distinct from its administrative phase. Though each complements the other, different personnel are needed for each.

Educators are chosen for their teaching ability, professional training, and experience. Education is concerned with standards of instruction which will implement the curriculum, inspire the teacher, and instruct the student. Therefore, educational work must of necessity be carved out by a well-trained teaching staff.

In the staff-line relationship, the Sunday school teacher will relay his need to the departmental superintendent. If the departmental superintendent needs help, he should seek the advice of the general superintendent. If further consideration is needed, the general superintendent should refer the matter to the pastor, director of Christian education, or perhaps the chairman of the Christian education board. As each individual keeps in mind the ultimate objective of bringing people into Christlikeness, the operation of the organized Sunday school will be fruitful.

PATTERNS OF ORGANIZATION

Sunday schools generally are organized into several divisions and then divided by departments or grades.

DIVISIONS

The four main divisions of the Sunday school are determined by periods of life:

Preschool	Birth through five years of age
Elementary	First through sixth grade
Youth	Seventh grade through high school graduation
Adults	College age and older

DEPARTMENTS OR GRADES

The two most common units of the contemporary Sunday school are the department and the grade, an organizational pattern which has been thoroughly tested and generally accepted. Grouping is a perfectly natural procedure by which students of like age, interest, or school grade are put together in classes.

When different classes are provided for each school grade it is called *closely grading*. When several grades are grouped together into a department the logical term is *departmental grading*.

The following departmental plan has proven satisfactory and become widely accepted.

Sunday School Departments	School Grades	Ages
Cradle Roll		Birth - 1
Nursery		2 - 3
Kindergarten	Kindergarten	4 - 5
Primary	1 - 3	6 - 8
Junior	4 - 6	9 - 11
Junior High	7 - 8	12 - 13
Senior High	9 - 12	14 - 17
College/Career	College	18 - 24
Adult		25 and over

There is a distinct advantage in maintaining separate departments of classes for the students in the junior and senior high school. The greatest number of students fall away from Sunday school between the ages of thirteen and sixteen.

During tnese impressionable years, good teachers, well-organized departments, and challenging curriculum materials must be provided.

A new problem in the late twentieth century is adult dropout. This is most common with newly-married young adults whose busy schedules and new responsibilities compete with earlier church loyalties. Many churches have found *elective grouping* by topic rather than age grouping to be effective in the adult division.

Some Sunday schools still operate a traditional extension ministry called the Home Department. Members who cannot attend regularly because of age, illness, home responsibility, employment, or other reason should not be denied the ministry of the Sunday school. They need a church fellowship and a sense of belonging, perhaps even more than if they were regular attenders. The Sunday school should be organized to activate their interest. The people who are unable to attend may be invaluable in their prayer support and other ministries adapted to their individual abilities and interests.

In organizing the Sunday school into departments, it may be necessary to estimate the enrollment of each. Conditions vary in different communities. In one, younger children may predominate. In a college town, the college and career group might be abnormally large. But on the average, the percentage of enrollment in the departments will look something like this:

Department	Ages	Percent
Cradle Roll—Nursery	Birth - 3	7
Kindergarten	4 - 5	8
Primary	6 - 8	10
Junior	9 - 11	10
Junior High	12 - 14	10
Senior High	15 - 17	10
College/Career	18 - 24	10
Adult	25 and up	35

Were Christian education nothing more than imparting information, the work of the teacher would be sufficient. But since worship and creative involvement are also vital, suitable provision should be made for programs and activities that will be appropriate for the various age groups. It is neither necessary nor desirable for the entire school to assemble for opening and/or closing services. Each department or grade should have a program that is correlated with its lessons.

For the promotion of common interests and enthusiasm, the entire school might assemble for special days, such as Rally Day and Children's Day. These occasions need not interfere with the educational program of the school and they may help to unify the total church program.

PROCEDURES FOR ORGANIZATION

Unless the Sunday school is well organized and enthusiastically supported, it cannot be expected to succeed. Without constant attention, even a well-organized Sunday school can fall into a chaotic and disorganized condition. To conserve good organization it is helpful to preserve departmental lines, require regular reports, and conduct staff meetings.

PRESERVE DEPARTMENTAL LINES

Departments should not be combined once they are established. Students should be promoted from one department to another as soon as they complete the required number of years or grades. As a general rule teachers should not, however, be transferred from one department to another but should specialize in the age group for which they are best fitted.

REQUIRE REGULAR REPORTS

No assignment should be made or task committed without provision for a report. The staff member must know the definite time, place, and type of report he will be required to give. Nothing dignifies a task and quickens its execution more than the fact that its performance must be reported. To assign a task and then ignore it, creates the impression that it is of little consequence.

CONDUCT STAFF MEETINGS

Effective organization is not possible without regular praying and planning. Pray for spiritual power and wisdom. Plan for intelligent, effective effort. A church-related organization cannot be successful without regular meetings. The superintendent has a right to expect members of his staff to cooperate in monthly meetings for instruction, inspiration, and planning.

SUMMARY

In order for Sunday school to be effective, good organization is vital. A well-organized Sunday school develops teamwork within its staff, identifies each person's responsibilities, provides for efficient teaching, clarifies the purpose of the overall program, focuses the aim and direction of all teaching and learning, enlists talents of all members, and encourages community outreach.

A basic step in organizing the Sunday school is establishing divisions. Even in the smallest schools, at least four basic divisions are used: preschool, elementary, youth, and adult. Most schools subdivide these groups into smaller departments and grades in order to better meet the needs of their students. A well-organized Sunday school of average size usually includes at least nine departments: cradle roll, nursery, kindergarten, primary, junior, junior high, senior high, college/career, and adult.

Three procedures that help keep a Sunday school on the road to success are: preserving departmental lines; requiring regular reports from teachers and leaders; and conducting meetings.

REVIEW AND DISCUSSION QUESTIONS

1. Briefly define Sunday school organization.
2. Name at least seven benefits to be derived from organization.
3. How are each of these benefits evidenced?
4. Define staff-line relationships and show how they operate.
5. What are the basic divisions of the Sunday school?
6. Name nine departments of the Sunday school with their corresponding ages and grades.
7. Suggest three ways to conserve good organization.

APPLICATION ACTIVITIES

1. Diagram your Sunday school organization, showing the relationship of the general leadership to the departmental leadership and the various departments and classes.
2. After examining Sunday school enrollment and attendance records, show how departments and class grading can be expanded if additional membership were brought into your Sunday school.

RESOURCES

Brown, Carolyn C. *Developing Christian Education in the Smaller Church.* Nashville: Abingdon Press, 1982.

Graendorf, Werner C., ed. *Introduction to Biblical Christian Education.* Chicago: Moody Press, 1981.

Sanner, A. Elwood and Harper, A. F. eds. *Exploring Christian Education.* Kansas City, MO: Beacon Hill Press, 1978. Chapter 13.

Leaders Needed

3

The success of a well-organized Sunday school depends largely upon those who administer its plans and policies. Failure frequently results from the spiritual unfitness of the Sunday school staff or their lack of leadership preparation.

Leaders and teachers must be chosen carefully and thoroughly trained for their tasks. Most local churches and Sunday schools have clearly defined methods prescribed in their bylaws or denominational handbook for electing leaders and teachers.

Several basic plans have been used successfully. Often Sunday school leaders are appointed by the board of Christian education, subject to approval by the church board. In some churches, the church board appoints the leaders or they are elected by the Sunday school membership or by the congregation. Other Sunday schools may elect the major leaders and authorize the superintendent to appoint his cooperating staff members. Teachers may be chosen by the board of Christian education or appointed by the superintendent, director of Christian education, or pastor.

The local needs and situation will determine the method used, but some general guidelines should be observed. Specific terms of service, clear lines of authority and responsibility, and personal invitation are all essential. The usual mediating body between the Sunday school and the church board is the board of Christian education (see E.T.T.A. text *Church Educational Ministries,* chapter 12).

PASTORS AND SUNDAY SCHOOL

The pastor is the spiritual and inspirational head of the Sunday school. He can do more than anyone else to inspire unity between church and Sunday school. He should take a definite interest in the Sunday school, developing and encouraging the faithful leadership of consecrated laymen. The pastor has responsibility in four areas: evangelism, visitation, teacher training, and installation.

EVANGELISM

Ultimately, Sunday school teachers will personally carry out most of the evangelism in the Sunday school, but someone must instruct them in the methodology and process. In addition to training teachers in evangelism, the pastor may also be involved in teaching a membership or new converts' class.

VISITATION

Lay people may serve as church or Sunday school visitation workers, but their calls cannot take the place of the pastor's. "A home-going pastor makes church-going people." The pastor who constantly emphasizes Sunday school in his visits will discover that its enrollment, attendance, and general interest are greatly improved. This will also strengthen the entire church program.

TEACHER TRAINING

The pastor should actively encourage a leadership training program, although he need not be the actual instructor. His vision will help promote the training of teachers and leaders, and the entire staff will likely cooperate.

INSTALLATION SERVICE

The dignity and responsibility of all the Sunday school staff members will be greatly enhanced if they are formally and publicly installed as leaders. The pastor should conduct an impressive service of installation and dedication at the beginning of the Sunday school year.

DIRECTORS OF CHRISTIAN EDUCATION AND SUNDAY SCHOOL

Churches continue to search for directors of Christian education who know God's Word and understand how to teach it in the church. Their qualifications, like those of the pastor, must be very high. Leadership ability and relationship to the Lord Jesus Christ are essential. Where it is not possible or desirable to have a paid professional director, the educational program may become the work of a lay director. Once a person has been assigned the position of director of Christian education, these varied activities should be performed:

CORRELATING

Correlation refers to the way all the various educational ministries of the church function in harmony. The Sunday school, usually the largest of these programs, must be properly correlated with other church ministries.

DEVELOPING

The success of the Sunday school depends largely upon the effectiveness of its teachers and leaders. The director searches for leadership potential, recruits promising people for future staff, and conducts training programs which provide up-to-date motivation, materials, and methods.

ADMINISTRATION

The director takes responsibility for oversight of the total operation of the church's educational program. He must be constantly aware of procedures that are presently being used as well as those which are anticipated and will ultimately be involved in staff management. However, as administrator, he should in no way usurp the authority or responsibilities of other staff members.

The director must be aware of staff facilities and materials at all times. He will pay particular attention to clearly defining and communicating the responsibilities of each staff member. He is not necessarily a specialist in each area, but his speciality is to train leaders to fulfill their individual functions, and to work together as a team.

TEACHING

The director is a leader of leaders and a teacher of teachers. His teaching responsibility lies largely in the development of leadership. He may be called upon at times to teach particular units of study, however, his major activities involve the observation, evaluation, and overall supervision of the teachers. He should be considered a resource person, who strengthens the quality and content of all teaching.

COUNSELING

The director is a shepherd to the Christian education staff just as the pastor is a shepherd to the congregation. He calls in the homes of those with whom he works where he may counsel both with groups of leaders as well as individuals, carefully interpreting the Christian education program to his associates. Through counseling he often solves problems that arise both in the classroom and among the teaching staff.

COMMUNICATING

Communication primarily involves the sharing of information which explains the church's educational program and builds enthusiasm for it. The director's vision for enlarging and improving educational ministries and facilities is infectious because it focuses on reaching and teaching people for the Lord. Communication may begin with the leadership including board members, superintendents, and teachers but ultimately must reach every church member and even interpret the educational ministry to the community.

SUPERVISING

Good supervision includes: relating the objectives of Christian education to the existing program; developing procedures for guiding and evaluating the existing program; working with the staff to encourage and develop skill in diagnosing difficulties; tracing inefficiency and prescribing remedies that will help the leadership realize results and success in meeting their objectives. The director of Christian education can only achieve this kind of suvervision by staying close to teachers and students on a regular basis.

SUPERINTENDENTS AND SUNDAY SCHOOL

The superintendent is administrative head of the Sunday school even when the ministerial staff includes a full-time director of Christian education. A director serving as Sunday school superintendent is counter-productive since it eliminates a valuable lay contribution. The average Sunday school superintendent may not be trained professionally for the educational task of the church, but he can use his administrative talents for advancing and improving the teaching ministry.

QUALIFICATIONS

The Sunday school superintendent is one of the most important lay leaders in the church. He should not be burdened with other offices and tasks. In addition to the basic spiritual qualifications of every church leader, he should be: organized, progressive, aggressive, enthusiastic, people-oriented, and efficient.

Organized

The task of leadership and administration requires clear-cut organization of time and ability. The superintendent, like other church leaders, must be able to use all resources effectively in the service of the Lord.

Progressive

The superintendent must keep ahead of the entire Sunday school. He must evaluate old methods without discarding them just because they are old. He must be alert to new methods but not accept them just because they are new. He is the visionary who sees what can be done and creates new ideas for helping the Sunday school be more effective.

Aggressive

The superintendent must be a person of action, never satisfied with the status quo, but vigorously producing new and greater achievements. He must take the initiative, establishing a team commitment to goal advancement in the Sunday school.

Enthusiastic

Sincere enthusiasm is one of the superintendent's greatest assets. The godly superintendent spreads a spirit of dependence upon the God of power. One zealous leader can inspire the whole team because enthusiasm is contagious in its positive influence.

People-Oriented

Along with his organizational and administrative responsibilities, the superintendent must maintain a vital interest in people of all ages. Disavowing special interests, he serves as the leader of all classes and groups in the Sunday school.

Efficient

The superintendent must be both administrator and leader. He is concerned for both the process and the people who are involved in the program. A knowledge of the program elements is necessary so that the operation is smooth and progressive. But it is equally necessary to know how to work with people in order to mold varying backgrounds, experiences, and interests into a harmonious working unit.

RESPONSIBILITIES

The superintendent should direct all plans for enlarging and improving the school. His major responsibilities are to think, to plan, and to execute what he has planned—delegating some responsibilities to the staff. He must keep the school growing both spiritually and numerically. The superintendent works with parents, board members, and all who need the ministry of the school.

The wise superintendent administers his work largely through the departmental superintendents who work directly with teachers and students. This does not lessen his responsibility, it only relieves him of departmental functions, allowing the superintendent to give personal direction to the general interests of the Sunday school.

While guiding the work of all general staff, the superintendent also inspires and directs the departmental superintendents, thus maintaining intimate and sympathetic contact with each department. Departmental superintendents and other members of the staff should be encouraged to help formulate Sunday school policies.

Any educational institution will function more effectively if there are regular meetings of its teachers. Discussions and conferences help the Sunday school leadership and teachers to work toward common goals, with unity of thought and action. The superintendent is responsible to plan, preside, and provide quality control for these monthly meetings.

With the soaring costs of church facilities, the superintendent is an important resource person in helping a congregation make the best use of its present space for an effective Sunday school program. However, when the most desirable facilities simply are not available, he may be called upon to assist in planning a new educational building or to devise other creative ways to carry out the teaching ministry.

As general administrator of the Sunday school, the superintendent must devise sound financial plans to provide for the general operational expense and needed additional housing and equipment.

ASSISTANT SUPERINTENDENT

The organizational structure of the Sunday school must be flexible in order to meet the needs and demands of the particular local situation. All Sunday schools, though, can benefit from the services of an assistant superintendent who assumes and fulfills specific responsibilities. He can handle membership promotion, recruitment of new staff, or follow-up of visitors. If highly trained, the assistant may supervise teaching methods or carry out responsibilities which involve equipment, publicity, or even evangelism and missions. In many churches the assistant is the heir apparent to the general superintendent and should therefore possess equivalent qualifications—high quality leadership, spiritual dedication, and administrative skill.

SUMMARY

Every well-organized Sunday school depends upon competent, dedicated, and spiritually-fit leadership. The Sunday school administration usually rests upon three individuals—the pastor, the director of Christian education, and the superintendent.

The pastor's role is that of inspirational and spiritual head of the Sunday school. His responsibilities usually are confined to four areas: evangelism—by training teachers to evangelize and by conducting classes for new members and converts; visitation—by encouraging Sunday school attendance; training—by promoting the training of leaders and teachers or by instructing a class himself; and teacher installation—by conducting an installation and dedication service for Sunday school leaders and teachers.

The director of Christian education has a more direct role in administrating the Sunday school. His responsibilities are: correlating of the various educational ministries into a harmonious program; developing the staff for all educational ministries; administrating the total educational program of the church; teaching the leadership; counseling with the educational staff; and communicating the educational program to the congregation, staff, board, and community.

The superintendent is the administrative head of the Sunday school. Because he is a key layman in the church he should be thoroughly grounded in doctrine. In addition, he should be organized, progressive, aggressive, enthusiastic, people-oriented, and efficient. His responsibilities include: directing all plans for enlarging and improving the Sunday school; working with departmental superintendents; guiding the work of all general staff; conducting teachers meetings; assisting the congregation to make the best use of educational facilities or planning new facilities; and devising financial plans.

Many Sunday schools include an assistant superintendent in their organizational structure. The assistant handles membership promotion, recruitment of new staff, and follow-up of visitors. Since the assistant superintendent is often in training to become the next superintendent, he should possess the same qualities as the superintendent.

REVIEW AND DISCUSSION QUESTIONS

1. In what ways can the church aid the Sunday school in its administration?
2. Why is a basic plan essential in electing leaders and teachers?
3. What attitude should the pastor take toward the Sunday school?
4. List the major responsibilities of a director of Christian education.
5. If a church has no director of Christian education, how can the educational program best be carried out?
6. List the qualifications of the superintendent.
7. Discuss the responsibilities of the superintendent.
8. What responsibilities can be given to the assistant superintendent?

APPLICATION ACTIVITIES

1. Analyze the leadership ability and methods of one Old Testament and one New Testament leader.
2. Thinking as a teacher, what services do you want a director of Christian education and/or Sunday school superintendent to offer you in order to make your ministry more effective?
3. Discuss the pros and cons of teacher election versus teacher appointment.
4. How long a term should a Sunday school superintendent serve? Why?

RESOURCES

Gangel, Kenneth O. *Competent To Lead.* Chicago: Moody Press, 1974.

———. *So You Want To Be A Leader!* Harrisburg, PA: Christian Publications, 1979.

———. *You Can Be An Effective Sunday School Superintendent.* Wheaton, IL: Victor Books, 1981.

Johnson, Douglas W. *The Care & Feeding of Volunteers.* Nashville: Abingdon Press, 1978.

Kilinski, Kenneth K. and Wofford, Jerry C. *Organization and Leadership in the Local Church.* Grand Rapids: Zondervan Publishing House, 1973.

Westing, Harold J. *The Super Superintendent.* Denver: Accent Books, 1980.

Sunday School as a Team Ministry

4

All Sunday school staff members are in Christian service and are expected to serve faithfully during the year. Spasmodic effort, irregular attendance, or irresponsible attitudes will fail to accomplish the goals of Christian education.

Each staff member is a key person, not just an assistant to the pastor or superintendent functioning only in the absence of another leader. The entire Sunday school team must be "workers together with God" (II Cor. 6:1).

The following positions are in addition to the superintendent and assistant superintendent presented in the previous chapter. These staff positions have been used in Sunday schools through the years and are still used in many schools today depending on their size. Although each of these positions is essential to an effective Sunday school, many smaller Sunday schools assign the responsibilities of some of the positions to other staff members to alleviate the problem of additional workers.

SECRETARY

As the source of information regarding progress and goals, an efficient secretary is invaluable to a successful Sunday school. He or she should be well informed about all details of the Sunday school, and able to answer any questions related to administration. If there is no assistant superintendent, the secretary may be the logical person to act as superintendent in his absence. This position sometimes requires more sacrificial service and receives less public recognition than any other. A good Sunday school secretary is characterized by neatness and accuracy, and has a genuine sense of the value of permanent records and files.

RESPONSIBILITIES

Every secretary has three well-defined responsibilities which are sometimes shared by assistants or departmental secretaries:

Record Minutes of Meetings

As recording secretary of all Sunday school meetings, the secretary should keep careful minutes of every session and perhaps assist the superintendent in preparing an agenda for the next meeting.

Handle All Correspondence

The secretary should be responsible for all correspondence which represents the Sunday school in its relationship to other organizations in the local church, the community, or the denomination.

Prepare Statistics

The secretary compiles, preserves, and reports the statistics of each Sunday school session, having received the details from the departmental secretary, superintendent, or teachers. These statistics involve the entire Sunday school, the departments, and individual students. Items of primary concern are constituency, enrollment, attendance, and offering.

TREASURER

Since the Sunday school is part of the overall program of Christian education, many churches feel that Sunday school expenses should be included in the church's budget. But for Sunday schools that keep their finances separate, a Sunday school treasurer is necessary.

The treasurer is entrusted with Sunday school funds. He is also responsible for providing full information about the Sunday school program and the cost of its operation. Through example, efficiency, and effort, the treasurer can be used of God to spearhead stewardship in the Sunday school.

RESPONSIBILITIES

The treasurer needs to know the financial procedures related to the operation of a Sunday school.

Handling Funds

Each Sunday the treasurer should receive the offerings after they have been checked and recorded by the secretary and should sign a receipt for these funds. He should pay all bills that have been properly authorized and secure receipts. Sunday school funds are not the treasurer's property. They are kept in trust to be used as directed by the proper authorities.

The treasurer should deposit all Sunday school funds in an account separate from his personal accounts. Careless treasurers have embarrassed themselves by putting Sunday school monies into the same pocket as their own. A separate, authorized bank account is absolutely essential.

Budget Preparation

Before the beginning of each fiscal year, the treasurer should receive a list of the anticipated supplies needed by each department. On the basis of these lists, he should work with the Sunday school finance committee and prepare an overall budget of current operational expenses, benevolences, and other adequate provisions to meet the needs of a growing school.

Reporting

Sunday school financial records must be prepared in an approved manner, so that they will be available and acceptable for annual audit. The published annual report and audit will encourage continued financial support by the Sunday school constituency, and will provide opportunity for testimony and reason for confidence in the business procedures used in the Lord's work.

MEDIA CENTER DIRECTOR

With the increasing demand and availability of multimedia materials for use in the Sunday school, many churches have established a media center. A consecrated, efficient media center director is an invaluable aid to the Sunday school teaching staff by meeting their needs with up-to-date multimedia teaching materials.

A media center director needs a working knowledge of current multimedia teaching materials and other educational aids. He will find it an adventure to investigate new materials, search out current trends, and keep informed on future developments in the ever-expanding field of multimedia equipment and materials. He should be in constant touch with all Sunday school staff members' needs and desires and be able to make suitable suggestions for filling them. If possible, the media center director should have some training or experience in this field.

The primary job of the director is to build and maintain the media center. In order to adequately finance the center, it should be included in the Sunday school or church budget. This amount can be augmented by personal contributions and special offerings.

Where there is no media center, one should be started. To initiate the project and to enlist the sympathetic cooperation of the entire church membership and its friends, a Sunday school might sponsor a media center "shower." The director should consult with staff members and make a list of a wide variety of learning materials needed for all ages and interests—filmstrips, overhead transparencies, records, books, flannelgraphs, teaching pictures. He might then distribute this list to all the church membership and friends and suggest that each family select one item to contribute to the new center. This should get the new media center off to a good start. Then each year new materials could be added.

The media center director should endeavor to keep all staff members informed on the materials available and how they are used. Many teachers are not familiar with all the newest materials and techniques but would be willing to try them if they received some instruction on their use and were kept informed of their availability.

The media center director should have adequate authority to acquire new materials for the center, see to their proper cataloging, and supervise the scheduling of their use. To accomplish this, the director should enlist the active support of the pastor, the superintendent, and other leaders.

This important resource person can perform a valuable service to the teaching staff by supplying up-to-date and relevant curriculum supplements. To perform this duty the director should be kept informed of the content of future lessons and might even be provided with copies of the instructor's guides.

MISSIONS COORDINATOR

Although missionary education should be carried on in all the educational programs of the church, the Sunday school is usually more involved in missions than any other educational ministry. For this reason, the Sunday school staff needs a missions coordinator.

The missions coordinator will see that missionary education

is taking place in the Sunday school classrooms. He will also provide current information about the missions that are being supported by the Sunday school. Since he is responsible for the missions program of the Sunday school, he should also be a member of the church's missions committee.

MUSIC COORDINATOR

Though an integral part of praise and worship, good music does not just happen. When used effectively, it will help build and maintain a successful Sunday school.

The music coordinator must work with the department superintendents and teachers to provide their students with meaningful musical experiences. Although musical training and experiences are valuable assets, they are not necessities for the music coordinator. He should, however, at least have a knowledge of and an appreciation for the best in Christian music. His main responsibility is to see that a coordinated program of music is carried out in the classrooms of the Sunday school. To do this, he will need to direct in the selection of graded hymnals and songbooks with the help of an appointed committee of Sunday school staff. Since he is responsible for all the music used in the Sunday school, he should be a member of the church's music committee.

Each department needs its own pianist and song leader. The music coordinator should have a file of all church people with musical talent upon whose services he may call.

DEPARTMENTAL LEADERS
DEPARTMENTAL SUPERINTENDENT

The departmental superintendent's responsibilities usually are delegated to him by the general superintendent. Like the general superintendent, he is basically an education administrator, but is responsible for the program in one department.

The departmental superintendent is responsible for classroom supervision, allocation of materials, and providing leadership in every activity related to the educational program of his department. As director of an important and distinct unit of the Sunday school, he should plan activities that will strengthen the unity and vitalize the personnel of the entire department. At the same time he must always remember that his work is part of the church's total program of Christian education.

Qualifications

The departmental superintendent is a specialist—thoroughly familiar with the characteristics of his particular age group. As he encourages the teachers and assistant teachers in his department to know and understand the age group with which they work, he should also be familiar with the characteristics of those leaders with whom he serves.

All the qualifications of a general superintendent are applicable to the departmental superintendent as well.

Responsibilities

While related to the general organization of the Sunday school, the departmental superintendent should be granted freedom to promote the plans and programs of his own department. He should represent his department at all meetings of the Sunday school staff and help establish the operational policies of the entire school.

Departmental worship programs have virtually replaced general opening exercises of the entire school. Music, prayers, Bible reading, stories, missions, and special emphases should be correlated with the lesson of the day and adapted to the understanding, needs, and participation of the students. Careful study and practice must be given to the preparation of these services. Securing assistance and cooperation from the teachers helps create a worshipful atmosphere.

Departmental teachers and other staff members should confer at least once a month to discuss problems of an administrative or educational nature. The departmental superintendent should set up a detailed, realistic agenda and provide actual leadership for these conferences.

The efficiency of the Sunday school and its total educational program will be increased if each departmental superintendent understands and does his job well. He should be familiar with current educational principles, curriculum resources, age characteristics, and evaluation materials.

Motivation is as important to the effectiveness of the departmental organization as it is to the teaching-learning process of the classroom. The superintendent will endeavor to encourage the teachers and other staff members of his department. Teacher morale can be uplifted most effectively by a positive attitude and desire to help them; the value of the departmental staff conferences; and the departmental superintendent's enthusiasm.

DEPARTMENTAL SECRETARY

Each department often has its own secretary whose functions are similar to those of the general secretary but on a departmental level.

The primary responsibility of the departmental secretary is the maintaining of individual records on all students in the department. He should record student absences and encourage teachers to faithfully follow up absentees. The departmental secretary will also report all attendance figures to the general secretary who maintains the permanent records for the entire Sunday school.

The departmental secretary assists in procuring and distributing materials. He should attend the monthly departmental staff meeting to communicate to the teachers the value and purpose of records in the total Christian educational program.

SUMMARY

The well-organized Sunday school depends upon an organization that carries out its goals as a team. In the last chapter, the "captains and coaches" of the team (pastor, director of Christian education, superintendent, and assistant superintendent) were presented. In this chapter the rest of the team was introduced. These team members include the secretary, treasurer, media center director, missions coordinator, music coordinator, departmental superintendent, and departmental secretary.

The general secretary is invaluable to the successful Sunday school. A good secretary is characterized by a genuine sense of the value of permanent records and files. The secretary usually performs three important functions: recording the minutes of meetings; handling all correspondence; and preparing statistics.

For Sunday schools that keep separate finances, the position of treasurer is important. Entrusted with the financial records and accounting of the Sunday school, he must be thoroughly acquainted with proper financial procedures and reporting methods. The treasurer's responsibilities include receiving and depositing offerings, paying bills, preparing a budget, and making up the yearly financial statements.

The media center director has become invaluable to the teaching staff of the Sunday school in recent years. The media center director provides a great service in providing and disbursing the various types of learning media available to the teachers.

Another position which contributes significantly to the success and development of the Sunday school is the music coordinator. This person is responsible for the selection and preparation of the music that is used in all Sunday school worship programs. Although it is not necessary for him to be an accomplished musician himself, he should be well informed on good, worshipful, and inspirational music.

The departmental superintendent acts in the same capacity as the general superintendent only on a single department level. Therefore he should be a specialist in that age group.

The departmental secretary should possess the qualities of the general secretary and perform the same duties on a departmental level.

REVIEW AND DISCUSSION QUESTIONS

1. Name the qualifications and responsibilities of the general secretary.
2. Outline a Sunday school treasurer's responsibilities.
3. Why should Sunday school financial records be audited annually?
4. How does the selection of good music contribute to Sunday school effectiveness?
5. What are the qualifications and responsibilities of a music coordinator?
6. Name the qualifications and responsibilities of the media center director.
7. What is the function of the missions coordinator?
8. Compare the functions of the departmental superintendent to those of the general superintendent.

APPLICATION ACTIVITIES

1. Prepare a brief handbook for Sunday school leaders including the qualifications and responsibilities of each leader and staff member, and a personal checklist of activities in which they should be involved.
2. Prepare your own program for establishing a media center in your church. Plan what materials should be included in a well-stocked media center and decide how these materials will be obtained.
3. Endeavor to show either by chart, diagram, or written explanation the relationship or benefit of each of the positions described in this chapter with one another. Show how each position needs to work together to provide an effective instructional program.

PERSONAL CHECKLIST

Because I am interested in the Sunday school, I

_____ Pray daily for the pastor, leaders, and teachers.

_____ Attend regularly and on time every Sunday.

_____ Study my Sunday school lesson (even if I'm not a teacher), so that the class period may be most profitable.

_____ Visit absentees and prospects and invite them to attend Sunday school.

_____ Volunteer to serve as leader, teacher, or staff member.

_____ Take teacher training courses to increase the effectiveness of my Christian life and witness.

_____ Am loyal, friendly, and zealous in promoting the Sunday school.

_____ Support the financial program of the church and Sunday school.

_____ Do my part to help create a sense of reverence, worship, and praise.

_____ Am a Sunday school enthusiast every day of the week and seek to glorify Christ in everything I do.

RESOURCES

Brown, Lowell E. and Reed, Bobbie. *Your Sunday School Can Grow.* Glendale, CA: Regal Books, 1974.

Gangel, Kenneth O. *The Effective Sunday School Superintendent.* Wheaton, IL: Victor Books, 1979.

Schaller, Lyle E. *The Multiple Staff and the Larger Church.* Nashville: Abingdon Press, 1980.

Schaller, Lyle E. and Tidwell, Charles A. *Creative Church Administration.* Nashville: Abingdon Press, 1975.

Training the Team

5

A well-planned, carefully-executed, long-range training program is a proven method for building a successful Sunday school. No Sunday school is really fulfilling its purpose unless it has effective teachers and productive students. Training teachers will accomplish both.

UNDERSTAND THE PURPOSES AND PROCEDURES OF TRAINING

PURPOSES

The purpose for the training of teachers is the improving of teaching quality. Jesus training his disciples is the model.

One of the goals of the Sunday school should be to keep up with advances in the field of education. That is not to advocate chasing after fads and trends, but steady and noticeable development of the quality of teaching in all departments.

When a training program is properly carried out, other peripheral benefits will result. Motivation on the part of students will be elevated. When students are motivated, numerical growth usually follows. A greater interest in evangelism and missions usually results when teachers become involved with training courses that require studying the Word of God.

PROCEDURES

Most Christian education programs in the local church are effectively expedited by their own people, trained by capable leaders to do the educational task to the glory of God. A serious-minded believer, indwelt by the Holy Spirit, can through effective teacher training, become a capable Sunday school teacher. The salvation and spiritual growth of many people depend on the supply of trained teachers to faithfully present the truth of God.

Training programs must be geared to the needs and resources of a local situation. In some areas, churches find it necessary to develop their own program, but where possible, cooperation in a community teacher training program offers much wider exposure to classes and probably a higher level of instruction.

Regardless of the schedule, teacher training must be done—whether weekly, monthly, or annually, whether alone or in cooperation with other churches, whether on Sunday or during the week—it must be done. But the big question frequently asked is, "How do we start?"

Starting a teacher training program is usually sparked by a leader with vision. Such a person with responsibility for Sunday school teacher training can revolutionize the church Christian education program. Perhaps designated as an assistant superintendent, he should be responsible for all phases of teacher training, this being his major Christian education contribution. He should encourage individual teachers. He should schedule in-service specialized departmental sessions and planning retreats for the entire Sunday school staff. Student observation and opportunities for guided teaching are also under his direction.

Once the program is initiated and the concept of continuous preparation is accepted by the Sunday school staff, timing of courses must be determined. Churches with successful teacher training programs have varied greatly in the degree of intensity of training. All successful programs, however, seem to have one characteristic similarity, they hold classes as frequently as the total Christian education program permits.

One pastor holds training sessions for six consecutive evenings at the same time each year. Another sets aside twelve mid-week sessions for teacher training. Courses are often presented as adult Sunday school electives or during a Sunday evening training session. Summer camps and vacation Bible schools provide an excellent opportunity. Unless a program is clearly and regularly scheduled, however, lasting effects are seldom obtained. Often the best time for teacher training is close to other scheduled church programs.

Training opportunities are multiplying as the concept of Christian education enlarges. Well-trained leaders and teachers supply the dynamic for improved Sunday schools. Under the anointing of the Holy Spirit, they open the door for a more effective ministry.

USE ADEQUATE MATERIALS FOR TRAINING

As indicated earlier, one key element in a successful Sunday school is the training of leadership. An important ingredient in carrying out a successful program of teacher training is the quality of the training materials used. Better materials have never been available for training Christian education leadership than in the last two decades of the twentieth century.

DENOMINATIONAL MATERIALS

Many large denominations have designed teacher training materials specifically geared to the educational curricula produced by their publishing house. Such programs usually focus on the particular theological and structural patterns of the denomination and aim exclusively at helping people become better teachers in the churches of that denomination. However, an increasing number of denominations now utilize the courses developed by the Evangelical Teacher Training Association which specialize in training Christian education leaders in the local church.

EVANGELICAL TEACHER TRAINING ASSOCIATION

E.T.T.A. offers courses that lead to both a Preliminary and Advanced Teacher Certificate. The Preliminary Program consists of six courses designed for a minimum of twelve class sessions. Three of the courses focus on the study of Scripture (*Old Testament Survey—Law and History; Old Testament Survey—Poetry and Prophecy;* and *New Testament Survey*) while three deal with methodology (*Understanding People; Understanding Teaching* or *Teaching Techniques*; and *Understanding Sunday School*).

Building upon the Preliminary Program is the Advanced Program also consisting of six courses designed in units of twelve weeks each and again with the same division between biblical and practical study. (*World Missions Today; Evangelize Thru Christian Education; Church Educational Ministries* or *Vacation Bible School; The Triune God; Biblical Beliefs;* and *Your Bible*)

When students successfully complete individual courses, award credit cards are issued. Upon completion of all six required courses in the Preliminary Program the student qualifies for the certificate. The same process is followed in the Advanced Program. E.T.T.A. certificates are internationally recognized for achievement of excellence in the field of Christian education.

Also available from E.T.T.A. is a non-credit program for training teachers during staff meetings titled, *Training When Meeting.*

E.T.T.A. courses are used in churches of over 50 denominations worldwide. Further information for starting a teacher training program may be obtained by writing directly to E.T.T.A.

UTILIZE SEMINARS, CONVENTIONS, AND CONFERENCES

Seminars, conventions, and conferences continue to be used of God for teacher training. They provide two very important ingredients in the overall leadership training process: inspiration and information.

SEMINARS

There are many types of seminars with a variety of sponsoring groups. Several Sunday school publishers send teams of experts to a city or a local church to conduct weekend workshops for church leaders. Church denominations will often host district, regional, or national seminars for the same purpose. Sunday school teachers are busy people so it becomes the task of the superintendent, assistant superintendent, or perhaps the director of Christian education to recommend what training programs are most useful for the staff. Many local churches feel that sponsoring all of its Sunday school teachers at one seminar or convention each year is a wise investment.

CONVENTIONS

The variety of Sunday school conventions defies description since they run from one to several days; attract less than a hundred people to several thousands; and operate on all kinds of geographical scales from a major urban area to a regional or national incorporation. The general sessions usually feature a speaker who can help Sunday school teachers understand the importance of their teaching ministry; while the workshop leaders provide practical help in new methodology and equipment. Numerous exhibits offer an opportunity to see the newest materials available.

STAFF MEETINGS

The monthly staff meeting is one of the most important single meetings of the Sunday school. What this group prays about, plans for, and implements will determine the Sunday school's success and overall effectiveness. All Sunday school leaders, teachers, and other staff members should attend.

DEPARTMENTAL SUPERINTENDENTS' CONFERENCES

At least twice a year the superintendent should meet with the departmental superintendents. They should present, explain, and promote the general policies, overall program, and the special emphases of their departments. Recommendations can be drawn up for presentation to the board of Christian education. Actions by the board can be studied and implemented. Effective conferences of departmental superintendents where plans and problems are discussed together give opportunity for interchange of ideas resulting in a good cooperative endeavor. This sharing of ideas will help the whole Sunday school function more smoothly, efficiently, and progressively.

EXECUTIVE CONFERENCES

Top leaders of the Sunday school should confer regularly. The Sunday school executive committee and the board of Christian education are not the same. The Sunday school executive committee is responsible only for Sunday school-related matters, while the board of Christian education has responsibility for the entire educational program of the church.

SUMMARY

The training of Sunday school teachers promotes a successful Sunday school. When teachers are trained, better learning results.

Although the main purpose in training teachers is to improve the quality of education, many times additional benefits result. Among these are: elevation of student motivation; growth in attendance; and greater interest in evangelism and missions.

The way a church trains its teachers varies according to its size, denominational affiliation, and location. Some carry on programs throughout the year, others through concentrated, limited-period institutes. Some cooperate with other churches while others prefer to handle their own program. However training is scheduled—it must be done.

Selecting the best teacher training materials helps to promote a successful program. Many denominations publish materials for their own churches, but an increasing number of churches prefer those which cross denominational lines and emphasize basic teaching principles.

Although holding teacher training classes within the local church probably constitutes the most effective means for training teachers, other less-formal resources are available. These include: seminars held by curriculum publishers and denominations; Sunday school conventions; monthly staff meetings; departmental superintendents' conferences; and Sunday school executives' meetings.

REVIEW AND DISCUSSION QUESTIONS

1. Why is teacher training important in the local church?
2. What is your church presently doing to develop leadership in its various Christian education programs, especially in the Sunday school?
3. What type of format in terms of time, length, and emphasis would be most useful for your particular congregation?
4. How could your church go about starting a teacher training program?
5. What is the major purpose of the staff meeting in the local church?
6. What is your church presently doing about Sunday school conventions? What should it be doing?

APPLICATION ACTIVITIES

1. Set up plans for a teacher training program in your church including methods of advertising and enrolling your own leaders, teachers, and prospective teachers.
2. Prepare a list of the regional or local conventions or leadership clinics which are available to your Sunday school workers. Begin to lay plans for encouraging attendance at these programs.
3. If you have had teaching experience, list areas of teaching where you feel you need definite help. Prepare a bibliography and/or other means which can aid in answering your questions.
4. List outside speakers whose areas of specialization will most benefit your teacher training program.

RESOURCES

Benson, Clarence. *Teaching Techniques.* Rev. ed. Wheaton, IL: Evangelical Teacher Training Association, 1983.

Gangel, Kenneth O. *So You Want to Be a Leader.* Harrisburg, PA: Christian Publications.

Sisemore, John T. *Rejoice, You're a Sunday School Teacher!* Nashville: Broadman Press, 1977.

Zuck, Roy B. and Getz, Gene A. *Adult Education in the Church.* Chicago: Moody Press, 1970. (Chapter 13).

Building for Ministry

6

The issues involved in determining church building design have changed drastically and seem to be in a constant state of flux. As a result, a church has difficulty making long-range plans for the design and development of a new educational unit to house its Sunday school. Nevertheless, units are being built; and God still lays upon the hearts of his people the value of building worship and educational facilities to the glory of Jesus Christ.

The concept of long-range planning has always been crucial in designing facilities for the church. Any church experiencing significant growth to the point that new classrooms, an addition to the present structure, or a completely new building will soon be needed, must plan carefully for the right facilities.

Key words when planning to build are: needs, purpose, design, and function. These, in turn, produce another key word, *ministry*. Every church and Sunday school is interested in ministry. A building is adequate and satisfactory only if it enhances the ministry that God's people are called to render.

NEEDS AND PURPOSES DETERMINE DESIGN

The question which determines whether to build and what to build is "What are the needs and purposes of the congregation now and what are they expected to be over the next twenty years?" It cannot be emphasized too strongly that building plans are dependent upon the needs and purposes of the church's educational ministry.

REMODELING PRESENT FACILITIES

By developing an overall plan of the areas involved, and often without tearing down walls, much better accommodations can be provided for Sunday school use.

Several types of accordion or folding walls are available. These do an adequate job of providing useable partitions. Suitable heavy drape materials also can be used to divide departmental space into classrooms. These materials may be pleated and made in double thickness for better sound absorption. Drapes cost less than accordion walls and, if hung on a proper track, serve practically the same purpose. Often the addition of acoustical ceilings and carpeting also help absorb sound.

ADDING TO EXISTING BUILDINGS

In some cases additions are very practical. Many older buildings have high side walls so that a two-story educational wing can be added and not be above the roof line of the old building. A balcony or closed second-story educational unit often can be installed at the rear of the sanctuary, with nursery facilities or classroom space below it.

Extensive remodeling is expensive. The cost per square foot is often higher than a new building, and the facilities may soon be crowded out again. Talk with an architect, contractor, or building consultant before considering an addition to the present structure. Preparing a master plan that includes projected educational needs will assure greater economy and better fulfillment of purpose.

PLANNING A NEW BUILDING

A good architect, designer, consultant, or engineer who understands the needs of evangelical churches is a valuable resource person. He should be thoroughly familiar with the church's functional needs, know architectural style, and to a great extent, the cost of building. Find someone who is known for thoroughness, integrity, and willingness to economize—one who will give the people what they really need. An architect cannot be expected to know the needs of a particular church. The building committee must know these and provide complete information for the architect who will translate them into a sound and well-designed building. Work for simplicity but with the possiblity of future expansion in mind.

DESIGN DETERMINES FUNCTION

The old question of which comes first, form or function, is as practical as it is philosophical. In reality, of course, the first step to be determined is the function of the educational program by clearly and specifically identifying its needs and purposes. Once these have been determined, the building can be designed.

If the Sunday school is divided into grades and departments and each is conducted as a separate unit, housing must include both departmental and classroom areas. The requirements for each vary greatly, depending upon the age of the students.

DESIGN FOR THE FUTURE

Many Sunday school facilities hardly provide for present enrollment, leaving little or no room for expansion. These church buildings make it almost impossible to experience significant growth in the Sunday school.

Attractive and adequate housing facilities appeal to the surrounding community. Sunday schools that demonstrate only a little faith when new buildings are erected often find their facilities overtaxed almost from the very start. It is wise to provide considerably more space than is necessary for the present enrollment. Provide for future expansion in an overall plan, both of the plot and the building. Be sure to get a draft or blueprint so that the plans will not be forgotten.

The many variables on the economic and demographic scene dictate the necessity for a seasoned professional to assist the church in projecting the kind of facilities it will need in the future.

DESIGN TO CONSERVE SPACE

In making an estimate of the size required for Sunday school facilities figure about 25 square feet for each child, and 10 to 12 square feet for each young person and adult. Under normal conditions, practically equal areas of floor space should be allotted to the various children's and youth departments. To adequately provide for a full elective program and larger numbers of adults at least three times as much space should be provided for the adult department as is given to any other.

DESIGN FOR ADEQUATE DEPARTMENTALIZATION

Information on space requirements may seem irrelevant to small Sunday schools, especially if they do not have rooms for departmental groups. If combined worship sessions are desired, the basement fellowship room, or Sunday school auditorium, may be used for all boys and girls up through the junior age. Junior highs through adults may meet in the church sanctuary or auditorium. If more rooms are available, further division should be between school-age and preschool-age children; then between youth and adults. As enrollment and facilities enlarge, each age group should be placed in a separate department to increase the effectiveness of the teaching-learning experiences.

The adult department is one of the most neglected in the Sunday school. Various age and interest groups within the adult department should have entirely different curriculum and lesson presentations. Many churches now conduct Bible study classes for young converts, young married people, business men and women, in addition to church membership preparatory classes, and teacher training. Good class rooms enable diversity of curriculum.

FUNCTION DETERMINES MINISTRY

What can be done in the buildings that are built is simply another way of defining the ministry of the church and the Sunday school. The process is a cycle: study the present ministry in order to determine if it is meeting needs and fulfilling objectives; reinterpret needs and revise objectives for the future; decide on design for additional facilities which will determine function and thereby activate a new approach to ministry.

MINISTRY TO CHILDREN

Plans should be made to have sufficient room for an expanding nursery and kindergarten. Then endeavor to enroll as many babies from the community as possible. If a cradle roll class for children from birth to age two is available, parents will feel free to bring them and the parents will also stay. Thus the early provision for infants becomes an effective way to reach the entire family. Also, provide a teaching nursery department for those over two. They are the nucleus of a great future Sunday school and church—a potential corps of Christian leaders.

In nursery and kindergarten, learning is often centered in interpersonal relationships. Children of this age should have relationships to a small group either as a class with an individual teacher or, if team teaching is utilized, for expressional activity following presentation of the lesson materials.

In the primary department a similar condition normally exists with class instruction becoming increasingly prominent. Classrooms are important to juniors and the size of classes in the primary and junior departments should generally be limited to eight to twelve students each.

MINISTRY TO YOUTH

Recent research has demonstrated that quality of leadership is the key to attracting young people to church and Sunday school. In the seventies youth was a rapidly growing segment of the population and new churches built at that time usually planned large areas for young people. More recent studies show that this is no longer the case. Effective and attractive facilities are still necessary to provide a full range of ministries to youth, but the amount of space needed may not be as great.

MINISTRY TO ADULTS

The age group to consider during the rest of the twentieth century will be the adults. All demographic studies show that the population is getting older and that middle and senior adults will dominate population trends. Some significant implications in planning for adult education will result. For example, facility design should include fewer stairs, wider doorways, and restroom facilities for handicapped people.

A renewed emphasis on small groups for fellowship and Bible study suggests not only the design of the rooms but also informality in surroundings. One of the key factors in design is multipurpose planning—using one space for as many activities as possible.

Building can be done with economy, in spite of the rising cost for housing and equipping today's Sunday school. This is accomplished by modern functional architecture. Planning ahead is imperative. Spur-of-the-moment decisions cost much more and usually do not result in satisfaction. Take time to check and recheck needs. Spend time in prayer. Decide on the right architect or engineer. Visit other churches and study their arrangements and use of materials. Be sure before building and prepare a master plan that covers the needs of the total church program.

SUMMARY

In order to provide the best possible educational program in the Sunday school, many churches find it necessary to build a completely new building or significantly remodel their present facility. But before doing either, a church should consider their needs, purpose, design, and function—or in a word—*ministry.*

When planning a building project, a congregation should ask itself, "What are our needs and purposes now and what do we expect them to be in twenty years?" Once the answers to these questions have been thoroughly considered, building plans can begin. At this point, a decision must be made whether to remodel the present facility, add onto the existing building, or plan a completely new structure.

When designing a significant building project, it is important to design for the future; design to conserve space; and design for adequate departmentalization.

A church's building should be built to carry out its ministry. Space should be provided for the various age groups according to the number of people in the group, and the kind of activities carried on within the group's program.

Recent studies show that the population structure is changing. Some time ago, the numbers of children and youth were high and programs centered on this section of the population. But more recently statistics indicate that in the near future adults will make up the largest section of the population. These statistics need to be considered in planning future church buildings.

For Sunday schools needing more or better facilities—something can be done. Even in poor economic times, God's people can work together to provide adequate facilities in which to teach God's Word. But before launching out into a building program, carefully evaluate your present needs, realistically plan for future growth, and fervently pray for guidance.

REVIEW AND DISCUSSION QUESTIONS

1. How do purposes and needs affect design?
2. What are two major principles to keep in mind in conserving space?
3. What is standard procedure in figuring space requirements for Sunday school facilities?
4. Discuss various ways in which a building can be remodeled.
5. What qualifications should describe a designer, consultant, or engineer employed to help plan a new building?
6. What is the best location for the educational unit of the church?
7. What are the suggested sizes of classes in the various departments?
8. What are advantages of having separate classrooms?
9. How do changes in population make-up affect planning Sunday school facilities?

APPLICATION ACTIVITIES

Though you may not be a member of the building committee, you will be a better Sunday school leader, teacher, or staff member if you know the facilities that are available in your building. The following check chart will provide a helpful class project.

1. General Information
   Sunday school enrollment   _____
   Sanctuary (auditorium) capacity   _____

Number of classrooms   _____
Future enrollment possibilities _____
Average attendance   _____
Church attendance   _____
Total capacity   _____

2. Specific Information   Yes   No

Are there enough classrooms? _____ _____
Are they well heated and ventilated? _____ _____
Are they light, clean, and attractive? _____ _____
Are there chalkboards and bulletin boards? _____ _____
Are there enough tables and chairs? _____ _____
Are they the correct size? _____ _____
Is there enough space to hang coats and hats? _____ _____
Is there good lighting throughout the building? _____ _____
Are there adequate restroom facilities? _____ _____
Are there sufficient exits? _____ _____
Is there adequate storage room? _____ _____
Is there a library? _____ _____
Is there a place to keep records and reports? _____ _____
Is parking space adequate? _____ _____
Are plans being made for improvement? _____ _____

RESOURCES

Graendorf, Werner C., ed. *Introduction to Biblical Christian Education.* Chicago: Moody Press, 1981. (Chapter 23)

Sanner, A. Elwood and Harper, A. F. *Exploring Christian Education.* Kansas City, MO: Beacon Hill Press, 1978. (Appendix I, pp. 475-483)

Schaller, Lyle E. *Effective Church Planning.* Nashville: Abingdon Press, 1979. (Chapter 2, pp. 65-92)

Sunday School Ministry: Evangelizing

7

The next three chapters are concerned with the ministry of the Sunday school which is perceived as "discipling." This ministry of making disciples incorporates three steps—evangelizing, edifying, and equipping. This chapter considers the first step—evangelizing.

The Sunday school is responsible to reach out into its surrounding community. The average Sunday school is lacking here. When a Sunday school conducts an effective evangelism program it reaches the entire community. In addition, it starts a multiplication process that can result in demonstrating the tremendous possibilities in Christ's command to go and make disciples.

PREREQUISITES FOR EVANGELISM

Every leader and teacher is responsible for reaching the Sunday school's constituency. This important task can transform the church, the community, the country, and the world. Several prerequisites are necessary for this process to catch fire in a Sunday school.

ENLARGED FAITH

The great conquests of the church are by faith. Those who believe God have "subdued kingdoms, wrought righteousness, obtained promises, stopped the mouths of lions" (Hebrews 11:33) and built great Sunday schools. "With God all things are possible" (Matt. 19:26).

VISION OF THE UNREACHED

Matthew 9:35 reveals that Jesus went about doing good,

reaching and teaching people. Matthew 9:36 notes that Jesus himself was moved with compassion as he viewed people, stating that they were as sheep having no shepherd. Where were the multitudes? Evidently, at that time, they were not in the synagogues. According to the words of Jesus, they were scattered abroad as sheep having no shepherd.

Where are the multitudes today? Evidently, they are not in the church. In fact, church buildings would not even hold all the church members if they came. Additional millions of people are not even enrolled in any Sunday school. A vision of the unreached people in your community and of their lost condition is absolutely necessary to move your church out into the community for Christ.

COMPASSION FOR THE LOST

The fact that Scripture records that Jesus was moved with compassion indicates that this was not merely a sudden or passing emotion. The Word of God presents this as our Lord's constant attitude and his invariable feeling toward people. In order for a church to reach its constituency, its leadership must recognize the need of people outside the church to accept Christ as Savior.

The Christian compassion should match Christ's commission. A positive, strong desire to win people to Christ must begin in the lives of those leading the Sunday school. When the leadership exhibits compassion and an awareness of people's need to accept Christ, this contagion spreads to the entire church membership. Truly, love is a constraining force. But this love involves not only a love *for* God, but a love *of* God for those who are outside his fold. When a church or a Sunday school stops seeking, it ceases growing.

UNDERSTANDING THE VALUE OF A PERSON

Sunday school leaders should be well aware of the value which the Lord placed upon the individual soul. The Word of God says that we are worth more than sparrows (Luke 12:7) and above the value of sheep (Matt. 12:12). Christ also used strong statements in an effort to help man understand the value of an individual soul. "For what is a man profited if he shall gain the whole world, and lose his own soul? Or, what shall a man give in exchange for his soul?" (Matt. 16:26). Considering the *faith*, the *field*, the *need*, and the *value* of a soul, reaching people is not merely a question of convenience, but on the basis of the Word of God, a divine mandate.

PREPARATION FOR NEW STUDENTS

The average Sunday school puts forth only meager, spasmodic efforts to increase its enrollment. Some schools conduct an occasional contest. Competition runs high for a time. Students strive to win a prize. Such methods accomplish a purpose, but they are not completely effective in building permanent enrollment and attendance.

Consecrated, carefully-prepared leaders maintain Sunday school enrollment and build attendance. When teachers commit themselves to evangelism, pray for its effectiveness, and are involved in its implementation, the Sunday school grows. Instruction in outreach techniques is almost as important for Sunday school teachers as instruction in teaching techniques.

Planning is essential if a church is to adequately handle an increased enrollment and attendance. A new or remodeled educational unit may be needed. For an outreach program to be successful over the long run, the church has to know what to do with the people who are contacted. The goal is making disciples, not contacting visitors.

PERSONNEL INVOLVED IN EVANGELISM

Present-day evangelicals stress the importance of regular church attendance. It is a major step toward successful evangelistic effort. An early contact with the Sunday school makes it easier to win an adult for Christ. But tragically only twenty percent of students are converted while attending Sunday school. Lack of evangelistic fervor is partly to blame, but the home and the church must assume equal responsibility for this lack of success. However, encouragement comes in knowing that the comparatively small fraction converted in Sunday school eventually constitutes three-fourths of our church membership. The other fourth is largely made up of adult converts who at some time were under the ministry of the Sunday school.

THE PASTOR

The pastor must be committed to Sunday school evangelism. This phase of his educational leadership should take priority. Though many Sunday schools seek to grow, most have no systematic evangelistic emphasis and effort. The pastor, in cooperation with every member of the Sunday school staff, should prepare a practical, perennial program, providing for vital relationships with parents, teachers, the school, and the church membership class.

As a representative of the Sunday school, the pastor introduces parents to those spiritual elements which nourish the growing child and prepare him to become a believer in Christ. In his visitation, the pastor shares the problems of the family and carries their burdens in prayer. He encourages parents to live their Christian faith in the family's everyday experiences.

Next to his ministry with the parents, the pastor works with the Sunday school teachers. The teacher holds the key to effective evangelism. Teachers who first win the confidence of their students can then guide them into spiritual matters. This is especially true in the teenager, who is sometimes reticent or unwilling to confide in his parents.

The pastor's responsibility, however, only begins with evangelism. He should receive a list of the names and addresses of all who make decisions for Christ. Then, as soon as practical, the pastor should personally interview these people. In this way, he can answer their questions or doubts, and ascertain their comprehension of their decision for Christ. In these class sessions he will present a well-rounded study.

THE PARENTS

In every generation, fathers and mothers hold the key to the evangelism of their own children. When parents possess genuine spiritual leadership, their children will accompany them in church and many will make early decisions for Christ.

THE TEACHER

In order for teachers to succeed as evangelists, they must be trained and prepared. Teachers must know that God has called them to win the lost. They must be trained to perform their task efficiently and enthusiastically. Teachers should know the steps to be followed in leading students to Christ.

Teachers should keep a notebook with a separate page for each student. On the page the teacher will record the student's name, address, school grade, birthday, picture, phone number, home life, hobbies, ambition, and spiritual progress. This is a convenient prayer reminder and helps to make prayers more specific.

To be soul-winners, teachers must first be people-winners. They must win students' respect. They must enter into the students' lives and seek to share with them.

The teacher's approach to the class is that of a friend. He is interested in the individual and in the group. Conversation with the students as they assemble encourages friendship and helps to win their confidence. Most educators feel that the most important time teachers spend with their students is when they first arrive. For this reason the teacher should be the first one there.

PRODUCTIVITY OF EVANGELISM

Three elements can be identified in developing a productive program of Sunday school outreach—prayer, godly living, and biblical methodology. If these three elements are kept in proper balance and priority, an outreach program will be successful.

PRAYER

The most important ingredient of effective Sunday school evangelism is a praying church. Every chapter in the book of Acts contains either a prayer or the record of a prayer meeting. Prayer is no less important for the people of God today.

When teachers pray for their students and tell their classes they are praying for them and why, Sunday school students are won to Christ. If only one thing can be done about Sunday school outreach, let it be a sincere and systematic program of prayer.

GODLY LIVING

Good teachers will not limit their ministry to teaching on Sunday morning. They know that they cannot win their students simply by what they say. Students need to observe consecrated Christian lives. The old adage declares, "You speak so loud by what you are that I cannot hear what you say."

Sick Calls and Friendly Visits

When someone is ill he appreciates every attention that is shown, and because he has fewer outside interests, he is most amenable to instruction. Calls on a sick or shut-in student will do more to win his love and respect than any amount of formal instruction. Moreover, visits to the home will give the teacher a first-hand knowledge of the environment in which the student lives and a better understanding of how to reach the student.

Social Events

Students are more easily won by a teacher who participates in their social events. It is no waste of time to spend an evening or a Sunday afternoon with a class planning recreational programs and participating in them. One teacher of a fifth grade class took his students to camp and spent two weeks with them. He played with them, laughed with them, and ate with them. He spoke to them about Christ. Thirteen of the fifteen professed Christ and later joined the church.

BIBLICAL METHODOLOGY

The early church knew nothing of inviting visitors. Its people were evangelists on location wherever unsaved people crossed their paths. To be sure, now that churches have specific places and times of worship emphasis on evangelism takes place more often among the gathered church. The point here is not to judge whether that is right or wrong; but simply to observe it as a fact of contemporary evangelicalism and deal with it to the best productivity for Sunday school evangelism.

In addition to teaching God's Word, counseling, visitation, and informal contacts with students, evangelistic Sunday school teachers need to take every opportunity to design specific approaches to outreach.

Publicity is important because it prepares the way for personal contact. It is comparatively easy to establish a point of contact in a community that is well informed about the life and work of a growing Sunday school. House-to-house canvasses require a well-planned program of publicity and briefing on visitation know-how.

Many Sunday schools effectively carry out community census or canvassing programs. These Sunday schools begin by finding out who lives there and what their attitudes toward church might be.

Sunday afternoon is usually the best time to take a religious census. Best results are obtained when preparation for this ministry includes an appropriate sermon at the morning service. A dedication of workers at church in the afternoon—just before they take up their task—insures and encourages promptness, inspiration, and fellowship. Canvassers will increasingly realize the importance of their task and will delight in sharing the resultant blessing.

Canvassers should be instructed to record each contact's name, address, number and age of children in the family, and church preference (if any) on index cards.

A special committee should investigate and evaluate all information secured by the canvass. The committee should disregard any cards for students actually attending other Sunday schools.

Those expressing a preference for other Sunday schools could be referred to those schools. After these reductions, the bonafide constitutency is established. Classify the prospective students and families by departments and classes, contact them immediately for enrollment in Sunday school.

Every Sunday school teacher should recognize his strategic position as an evangelist. Sunday school evangelism is more fruitful where instruction in evangelism is required of all teachers. Sunday school evangelism should constitute a vital part of every teacher training program. Evangelical Teacher Training Association offers a special course entitled *Evangelize Thru Christian Education.* The church contributes to evangelistic success by providing training for Sunday school teacher-evangelists. But even if teachers have been trained in personal evangelism and are consecrated to the soul-winning task, the pastor's personal interest will be reflected in the attitude of the teachers. Fall planning conferences or retreats should include an opportunity to encourage teachers to "do the work of an evangelist."

SUMMARY

The Sunday school is responsible to reach out into its surrounding community.

In order for a Sunday school to reach out, several prerequisities are necessary: a faith that believes growth can be accomplished; a vision for the unreached in the community; a deep compassion for those who do not know the Lord; an appreciation of the value of a person; and a building prepared to handle an increased enrollment.

In order for a Sunday school's outreach program to be effective, the whole staff must be involved—pastor, leaders, teachers, and (in the case of children) parents.

The pastor is responsibile to promote evangelism among his staff, in the congregation, and through personal contacts in homes. The pastor is involved in evangelism from an initial outreach program through a church membership class for the new converts.

Parents hold the key to winning their children to Christ. Surveys point out that the largest number of young people who accept Christ come from Christian homes.

The key to the Sunday school teacher's effectiveness as an evangelist is his rapport with his class. If he captures their respect and love, he has a greater chance to win them to Christ. Training in evangelism techniques will also increase the teacher's effectiveness as an evangelist.

For an outreach program to be productive, three elements are necessary: a praying church uplifting the program before the Lord; the godly lives of the evangelists; and biblical methodology in carrying out the visitation program.

REVIEW AND DISCUSSION QUESTIONS

1. How is regular church attendance related to successful evangelism?
2. Why should Sunday school evangelism be of interest to a pastor?
3. How can a pastor enlist the support of parents in evangelism?
4. Why should every teacher be trained in personal evangelism?
5. How is the teacher a key to Sunday school outreach?
6. How does publicity affect a Sunday school outreach program?
7. Why is Sunday generally considered the best time for canvassing?
8. Why is reporting of canvass activities essential?
9. Who is responsible for the information secured by the canvass?

APPLICATION ACTIVITIES

1. How would you lead a child to Christ? A young person? An adult?
2. Evaluate the program of evangelism in your church. What are its strengths and weaknesses?
3. Survey your last quarter's curriculum materials carefully to note at what point evangelistic opportunities were presented in your lesson materials. Then evaluate your reaction to these as you review what you did in class at that particular point. Also, examine the material for the forthcoming quarter, noting carefully those lessons which readily lend themselves to evangelism within the classroom.

RESOURCES

Coleman, Robert E. *The Master Plan of Evangelism.* Old Tappan, NJ: Fleming H. Revell, 1964.

Fisher, Wallace E. *Because We Have Good News.* Nashville: Abingdon Press, 1973.

Hendricks, Howard G. *Say It With Love.* Wheaton, IL: Victor Books, 1972.

Soderholm, Marjorie. *Explaining Salvation to Children.* Minneapolis: Free Church Publications, 1979.

Towns, Elmer L. *Evangelize Thru Christian Education.* Wheaton, IL: Evangelical Teacher Training Association, 1976.

Sunday School Ministry: Edifying

8

In the last chapter, evangelism was considered. Evangelism is the first step in Sunday school ministry. The second step is edifying, or building up in the faith. Sunday school ministry begins with reaching out into the community and confronting people with the truth of the gospel. Accepting this truth, however, is just the beginning. The Sunday school must be prepared to take this new person in Christ and teach him the things of the Lord. The Sunday school's responsibility rests primarily in carrying out the Lord's commission to "go and make disciples" (Matt. 28: 19 NAS). This process begins with the outreach program and is continued by building up those won to Christ—teaching them the Word of God.

PREREQUISITIES FOR EDIFICATION

Leaders and teachers must possess several qualities if they are to carry on the process of helping those who attend Sunday school grow up spiritually.

LIVES THAT REFLECT CHRIST

Anyone seeking to build up other believers must first influence them with his own life. While no one except Christ is perfect, teachers must be rooted and grounded in the faith themselves before they can lead others into spiritual growth.

Paul told Titus to be a *pattern* of good works (Titus 2:7). The word that is translated "pattern" literally means something a person would lay down and trace around to make a duplicate. He who seeks to help others grow in the faith needs to have a life that is worthy of being copied. People become more encouraged to live the Christian life when they see it being lived out in the lives of others.

TIME TO SPEND WITH THE STUDENT

One who is really intent on carrying out the Sunday school's responsibility to edify its constituency must be willing to spend time with those who attend. Looking at Christ's example reveals a 2-3 year time period of total dedication to twelve men. While Sunday school teachers cannot spend a 2-3 year period with their students, helping them build up their faith does require more than a one-hour-per-week commitment. The edification process demands getting to know the student both in class and in other settings as well. Building up students in the faith is sometimes more easily accomplished in an informal meeting during the week than in the structured atmosphere of the classroom.

Christ was a leader, teacher, adviser, and guide to those he discipled. But he was also their friend. John 15:14 expresses this in the words, "Ye are my friends." Sunday school teachers who have not become their students' friend probably have done little to build them up in the faith. But those teachers who become friends to their students find many opportunities to help them experience continual spiritual growth.

PERSONNEL INVOLVED IN EDIFICATION

The Sunday school's ministry of helping its members grow spiritually should comprise much of its educational program. Evangelism might be the initial objective, but edification should be the bulk of its ministry. Keeping this in mind, all Sunday school personnel should be committed to the spiritual development of their students.

PASTOR

The pastor, by virtue of his leadership role in the overall program of the church, encourages spiritual growth each week from the pulpit. Since the ministry of the church is also one of direct discipleship, the pastor is constantly concerned with building the faith of his entire congregation.

Parents have the strongest impact on the lives of their children. Therefore, the pastor should provide them with advice on building up their children in the faith. He should also counsel and pray with parents who need help in guiding their children's spiritual growth. If the pastor's own life is a shining example of what it means to be a follower of Christ, he will be a true edifier of men.

The pastor's responsibility begins with the program of

evangelism and continues with instruction classes for new converts. A well-rounded study of the Christian life and stewardship should be presented in these class sessions. In most churches, these classes initiate the process of growing in the faith and serve as an introduction to church membership.

PARENTS

As in the case of evangelism, Christian parents have the best opportunity to feed and nurture their children in the things of God. Their Christianity is constantly on display before their children's eyes. As pointed out previously, the majority of children coming from Christian homes accept the Lord through their parents' example. And it is also true that parents, through opportunities such as family devotions, can continue the process of discipling by helping their own children grow up in the faith. But in many Christian homes, devotional times are not part of the family's regular activities together and children often are not spiritually fed by their parents. So it then becomes necessary for the Sunday school to provide leadership for edification.

TEACHER

If the teacher is trained and prepared to be a soul-winner, he will probably also be instrumental in continuing to guide his students.

Here again it will be the teacher's life, rather than his words, which will be most effective in helping influence students toward spiritual growth. If the teacher is himself rooted and grounded in the Word of God, he will be more successful in helping students grow up in the faith.

The key to fulfilling the teacher's role in edifying students rests in his personal relationship with them. If he shows sincere concern for their growth in the Lord, they will respond. If he spends time getting to know his students outside of class, they will be free to express a desire to know more about the Christian life.

Above all, the teacher should not be phony. More will be accomplished by taking an honest approach to life. Even teachers are occasionally tempted and frustrated and their lives are not completely free from problems. Students appreciate teachers being open. Those who teach children might share how they felt while growing up. Students will feel close to the teacher whom they realize was once a child like them.

PRINCIPLES FOR PRODUCTIVITY

Three elements are imperative for developing a productive edification program in the Sunday school—prayer, knowledge of the Bible, and patience. If these three elements are found in the lives of teachers and parents, they will make a large contribution toward the program's success.

PRAYER

It has been said "When all else fails—pray." How much better for the principle to be "Before everything else fails—pray." The importance of this phase of the Sunday school's ministry cannot be stressed too much. The future of the church depends on a constant supply of mature Christians to carry on its ministries. The Sunday school's ministry of building up people in the faith needs support with prayer in general and departmental meetings of the Sunday school as well as in weekly congregational prayer meetings. As individuals in the church and Sunday school regularly pray for this important Sunday school ministry, many will be helped.

Scripture again and again points out the value of prayer in a discipling ministry. Throughout his ministry, Jesus prayed on behalf of those he led. Paul mentions many times that he was praying for the members of the churches he helped found.

Teachers who are involved in the ministry of edification should be people of prayer who are constantly bringing their students' needs before the Lord.

KNOWLEDGE OF THE BIBLE

Teachers who are seeking to help their students grow spiritually must themselves be students of the Word. Before helping to strengthen a new believer in the Christian life, Sunday school teachers themselves need to know the Bible—the sourcebook of the Christian life.

A three-fold understanding of God's Word is necessary for every teacher.

Doctrine

Teachers need a working knowledge of such great biblical doctrines as the Trinity, the incarnation and deity of Christ, and salvation. A firm foundation in the Word of God will help others deepen their convictions in spiritual matters.

Bible Background

The teacher not only needs to understand the Word but must also have a grasp of Bible backgrounds and history. This knowledge will strengthen his understanding of the biblical message.

How the Bible Relates to Life

A practical grasp of how the Bible applies to the problems and relationships of life is essential. A teacher must be able to point students to the place in the Bible where they can find the answer to the difficulties they face in life.

All three of these areas of Bible knowledge require constant study for teachers to be ready to build up others in the faith. The benefits from preparation in these areas will be evidenced in the spiritual lives of their students.

PATIENCE

When it comes to growth in grace—edification—patience is not just a virtue, it is a necessity. Students assimilate information, apply knowledge, and make it part of their everyday behavior at different rates. Because one student makes great strides toward growing up in the Lord and another barely takes a step does not mean the teacher is effective in one case and not in the other. The Lord works his plan differently with each individual. Perhaps tomorrow, next week, next month, or even next year the scene will be completely changed, but the end result will be spiritual growth. The Lord will produce results in his time.

SUMMARY

The second step in discipling a person for Christ is edifying—building him up in the faith.

Since this ministry is so vital to the life of the Sunday school, everyone needs to be involved. Valuable prerequisities for those leading the program are: lives that reflect Christ, time to spend with students, and a willingness to be a friend.

Three people are instrumental in a successful ministry of edification—the pastor, the parent, and the teacher. The pastor should be constantly helping his congregation grow in the faith from the pulpit, in home visitation, and in guiding the Sunday school staff. As with other ministries among children, the parents need to be involved in lending support to the program and in carrying out some of its aspects in the home. The teacher often is the most important factor in the success of the edification program. The teachers who are most successful in edifying their students have lives that illustrate their words, gain their students love and respect, spend time with their students outside of class, and are honest in relating their own shortcomings and failures.

Principles for productivity in an edification program are: prayer for and about the program; a strong knowledge of the Bible; and patience on the part of all concerned.

REVIEW AND DISCUSSION QUESTIONS

1. What is the primary responsibility of the Sunday school ministry?
2. Why must everyone in the Sunday school be committed to the program of edification?
3. Why must the edifier's life be rooted and grounded in the faith?
4. How can a teacher find ways to spend time with his students outside of class?
5. Why is it important for teachers to be their students' friend?
6. How can parents help their children to grow spiritually?
7. How can a teacher avoid appearing phony?
8. What three levels of Bible knowledge should the teacher have attained?
9. Why is patience so important for an edification program to be successful?

APPLICATION ACTIVITIES

1. Evaluate the quality of students presently being produced in your Sunday school. Are there evidences of maturing? Of growing spirituality? Of balance in Christian living?
2. Design a specific one-year edification program for your class. If you have a small class, you might be able to work on a personal basis with each student over the next year. If your class if large, you may want to design discipling partnerships whereby more mature class members work with less-advanced students under your supervision.

RESOURCES

LeBar, Lois E. *Education that is Christian.* Old Tappan, NJ: Fleming H. Revell, 1981.

Stedman, Ray C. *Body Life,* Glendale, CA: Regal Books, 1972.

Sunday School Ministry: Equipping

9

The Sunday school's ministry primarily is discipling students. The previous two chapters considered the first two steps in the process—evangelism and edification. This chapter deals with the third and final step—equipping for service. With this third step, the Sunday school's ministry is complete. Having reached out and won people to Christ and then built them up in the faith, the Sunday school needs to equip them to go out themselves and make disciples. This third step completes the cycle and prepares it to begin again.

PREREQUISITIES FOR EQUIPPING

In order for a Sunday school to carry on a successful ministry of equipping its constituency for service, several conditions must be evident.

STUDENTS WHO ARE MATURING SPIRITUALLY

In Ephesians 4, Paul clearly identifies the task of church and Sunday school leadership ". . . to *prepare* God's people for works of service, so that the body of Christ may be built up until we all reach unity in the faith and in the knowledge of the Son of God and become mature, attaining to the whole measure of the fullness of Christ" (Eph. 4:12, 13 NIV). Note the inseparable relationship between knowledge and behavior. We grow in knowledge, become mature, and thereby are equipped to perform works of service.

Knowledge has to do with information. In the case of Christian growth, information about the Bible and the truth about God and man lay the foundation not only for salvation, but for Christian growth. But simply having the knowledge does not produce changes in students' behavior. Students must believe what they have heard or learned in order to have it affect their lives. Then, because students believe certain things, they choose their values and begin acting within the framework of these values. This is the ultimate goal—students who are mature in Christ, who live according to biblical standards. When Sunday school students attain this level, they will be ready to be equipped for serving Christ themselves.

TEACHERS WHO ARE PATIENT

Church workers tend to gravitate toward glamour ministries, particularly those which will produce visible and immediate results. But those who have selected Sunday school teaching as their field of service know that it is a long-term, sometimes tedious, but always essential ministry. Teaching is central to the church's biblical ministry. Jesus himself was called the master teacher. In his post-resurrection appearance on the Emmaus Road, he expounded the Scriptures (Luke 24:27), and the central emphasis in his great commission is upon teaching (Matt. 28: 19). In Paul's list of gifts of the Spirit, teaching is permanently united with pastoral work: "He gave some . . . pastors and teachers" (Eph. 4:11).

As was mentioned in an earlier chapter, patience is essential to a teaching ministry. A student will not be ready to serve after reading through the Gospels once. Nor will a year of Sunday school totally equip him for service. Note how God has worked with his men and women through the ages. Moses spent forty years in the desert in addition to his forty years in one of the major urban centers of the world. The apostle Paul had a brilliant education in Greek culture and Hebrew theology but was set aside for preparation before he was useable by the Lord. The disciples struggled and failed for over three years before any real significant positive results of their ministry became evident.

God is not in a hurry to produce effective servants. He is patient with our failures, frustrations, and futility. Why then are teachers sometimes impatient for their students to attain spiritual maturity? Each person and each situation is different. Sometimes it requires trying various methods to see if they work. One teacher might find that discussion works best, while another might find students respond to role-play activities or buzz groups. Whatever methods attain the best results in producing student knowledge and behavior should be employed. To advance students from the level of knowledge to that of behavior takes reliance on the Spirit of God, dedication to study on the students' part, and use of helpful materials, training classes, counseling with others, and a great deal of prayer.

A SUNDAY SCHOOL THAT ENCOURAGES SERVICE

Some Sunday schools are satisfied with students who know Bible stories and can quote the Bible accurately. Other Sunday schools strive for a large attendance but little else. But for Sunday schools that are interested in carrying out their biblical mandate, Christian service must be stressed.

Sunday school has the greatest potential for acquainting students with opportunities for service and has within its own organization many possibilities for serving Christ. Sunday schools that provide opportunities for service throughout their own programs encourage students to participate in various service projects even while they are still spiritually immature. Students will most likely continue to be active in Christian service if they have been given opportunities to serve Christ while they are maturing in the faith. Members of the Sunday school from the youngest to the oldest can serve the Lord. Many spiritual seeds have been planted by primary children who explain Jesus' love to their friends. Juniors can serve their Lord by spreading the word about God's love in their school classes, on the playground, and at home. But these children, as well as youth and adults, seldom serve on their own. They need to be introduced to the possibilities and encouraged to fulfill them. Sunday schools that provide instruction and encouragement for service, both fulfill their objectives for ministry and reap the benefits in growth.

PERSONNEL INVOLVED IN EQUIPPING

It takes people serving Christ to influence others to become involved in Christian service. Keeping this in mind, the whole Sunday school team needs to work together encouraging students to get involved in Christian service.

PASTOR

The pastor's responsibility to Sunday school ministry as a whole is one of providing support and encouragement. His role begins with the program of evangelism, continues with instruction of the new converts' class, and climaxes with providing suggestions of areas where mature Christians can serve Christ within the framework of the local church.

The pastor is also the best model within the local church of a mature Christian who has chosen a career in Christian service. For this reason, he should make himself available for counseling any Sunday school student who has questions concerning full-time Christian service.

Above all, the pastor encourages his entire congregation, and Sunday school leadership in particular, to be involved in active Christian service.

PARENTS

The role of parents in the process of equipping children for Christian service is one of example. When children see their parents involved in serving Christ in many capacities, they are more likely to become involved themselves in Christian service. Many acts of Christian service can be done as family activities. Unfortunately, many of today's Christian families, who operate under the pressure of both parents working and full schedules of other activities, often find little time for each other and even less time for Christian service. This increases the Sunday school's responsibility to provide leadership in equipping students for Christian service.

SUNDAY SCHOOL STAFF
Leaders

The Sunday school leadership needs to work together to enlist every student in some form of Christian service.

In departmental and general staff meetings, the superintendents should stress with teachers and other staff members the importance of involvement in Christian service.

Sunday school leaders should also strive to involve as many people as possible in serving Christ within the Sunday school organization. Many jobs need to be done: teaching, assisting, playing instruments, and leading worship sessions. All these opportunities provide areas for persons to serve Christ. It is the leaders' responsibility to help people get involved.

Teachers

Involving students in Christian service is the ultimate objective of Sunday school ministry. The teacher is the prime motivator. But many teachers fall short in this part of their ministry. Reasons for this vary. Some teachers just don't have time to see that students demonstrate their faith. Others feel that they do not have the expertise to equip others for serving Christ.

Still others feel that most of their students are not mature enough to adequately serve the Lord.

Whatever the age-level, whatever the degree of maturity, students need to be involved in Christian service. Enlisting students in service projects usually calls for more than the one-hour-per-week class time. For young children to become involved in service projects, the teacher must accompany them or guide them as they work in a group or give individual students help in fulfilling their assignments. Time spent in equipping students for Christian service is never wasted.

Most Sunday school curriculum materials provide lesson-related suggestions for involving students in service projects. Teachers that utilize these ideas find that their students' spiritual experiences are broadened and their faith becomes more meaningful.

For some members of the Sunday school, the teacher may be the only model of a person serving Christ that they see. Students coming from non-Christian homes need to observe how to serve Christ. Teachers should show some special attention to these students and should encourage them to demonstrate their faith. Teachers who have become their students' friend will find it easier to equip them for service.

If there are students who seek to enter full-time Christian careers, expose them to all the possibilities. Enlist the aid of assistants, the media center director, the missions coordinator, and others to provide these students with information about full-time Christian service.

PRINCIPLES FOR PRODUCTIVITY

Three elements are important for making a program of equipping students to serve Christ more effective: challenging students to greater faith, conveying enthusiasm, and emphasizing further training.

CHALLENGE STUDENTS TO GREATER FAITH

When Christ equipped his disciples for service, he didn't give them a list of things he wanted them to do, nor did he threaten them. Instead, he showed his love for them by explaining that he was going to prepare a place for them. He said that he would send the Holy Spirit to help them and informed them of the privilege of prayer. He also conveyed warmth, personal interest, concern, and acceptance.

Christ's methods challenged that group of eleven men to go out and turn the world to Christ. Teachers using his methods can do the same for their students. After assuring students that Christ will be with them in all they do, give them responsibilities and increase these responsibilities according to the students' response. As students become involved, they will be motivated to do more. Place students in positions where they need to trust God and expose them to situations where their faith will be tested. When they succeed victoriously in small things, they will be challenged to do greater things.

For students who desire to read about other people who lived by faith, have books available that show how men and women have trusted God in times past.

CONVEY ENTHUSIASM

Enthusiasm is a great motivator. Sunday school students need to observe people who are enthusiastically living the Christian life and involved in Christian service. The teacher who relates how exciting living for Christ can be, greatly influences his students to enter Christian service. Speak to them of your own experiences and tell them of your triumphs in Christ's service. Also, bring other people into the classroom who will testify of the Lord's provision in their lives.

Above all, give students a purpose for serving Christ. Explain to your students that God wants to use them in meaningful ways.

EMPHASIZE FURTHER TRAINING

Equipping students to serve Christ in their lives can be done within the Sunday school and church program. For people who desire to serve in leadership capacities, further training is essential. This training can take many forms. For students desiring to fill lay leadership positions, training might take the form of correspondence courses or programs such as E.T.T.A. Those whose goal is serving in full-time Christian ministries—Bible school, college, or seminary training is essential.

Teachers in the youth department should keep themselves informed of good Bible schools and colleges so they can help their students make wise decisions concerning what school to attend. These teachers might also ask Christian colleges or organizations to send literature to their students or invite a representative from a local Christian youth organization or Bible school to speak to their teenagers.

SUMMARY

The Sunday school's ministry is not complete until students are fully equipped to serve Christ.

To accomplish this, several prerequisites must be evident: students must have reached a level of spiritual maturity; teachers must exhibit patience, not requiring that all students be ready to serve at the same time and in the same way; the Sunday school organization must encourage its constituency to become involved in Christian service.

A successful program of equipping students for service requires the entire Sunday school staff to work together as a team. It also needs the cooperation of the pastor and parents to be completely effective. As in other levels of Sunday school ministry, the teacher is instrumental in carrying out the program.

For a program of equipping students for Christian service to reach maximum productivity, three elements are vital: challenging students to greater faith, conveying enthusiasm, and emphasizing the need for further training.

REVIEW AND DISCUSSION QUESTIONS

1. Discuss the pattern of how knowledge becomes behavior.
2. How can Sunday school teachers develop patience?
3. Name some ways a Sunday school can stress Christian service in its program.
4. Why is the pastor important to a successful program of equipping students for service?
5. How can parents influence their children to become involved in Christian service?
6. What is the role of Sunday school leadership in carrying out the equipping ministry?
7. Give five sources of ideas for involving students in Christian service.
8. How can the Sunday school teacher challenge students to demonstrate greater faith?
9. Why is enthusiasm so important to a productive equipping ministry?
10. Name four ways students can further their education in preparation for serving Christ.

APPLICATION ACTIVITIES

1. Prepare an equipping program for your entire Sunday school or for a single class.

2. Design your own self-improvement program to help you become a better equipper of students for Christian service.

RESOURCES

Hadidian, Allen. *Successful Discipling*. Chicago: Moody Press, 1979.

Henrichsen, Walter. *Disciples Are Made—Not Born*. Wheaton, IL: Victor Books, 1974.

Hendrix, John and Householder, Lloyd. *The Equipping of Disciples*. Nashville: Broadman Press, 1977.

Wolterstorff, Nicholas P. *Educating For Responsible Action*. Grand Rapids: Eerdmans Publishing 1980.

Resources for Effective Teaching

10

Next to the Sunday school teaching staff, the most important factor that affects learning is the curriculum. Curriculum includes the subjects taught, their interrelationship, sequence, and development. Good teachers using a good curriculum create a school of high educational caliber. For churches that accept the Bible as the center of the curriculum in their Sunday schools, all the goals, materials, and activities must be built on the Word of God. God's Word will continually be applied to all age levels on the basis of current needs and problems.

CURRICULUM PHILOSOPHY

Some Christian educators use the term curriculum to include the materials used, the learning processes and experiences of the student, and the teacher's philosophy and methods. However, as used in this chapter, *curriculum* is limited to a course of study which leads to and accomplishes the basic aims of the Sunday school.

Curriculum is the complete, prescribed outline of studies for a particular group for a particular purpose. It is a means to an end, not an end in itself. Curriculum guides the student to accomplish educational objectives.

FUNCTION OF CURRICULUM MATERIALS

The materials used to implement the curriculum and to bring it within the learning experience of the student are included in the term *curriculum materials*. Such materials should aid in the presentation of the chosen curriculum. Teachers' textbooks, students' study books, visual aids, supplementary Scriptures, memory verses, and methods—all are defined as curriculum materials. Curriculum materials should include information, activities, and experiences specifically related to areas common to an age group. Because life is complex and each person must deal with it realistically, curriculum materials should embrace the home, church, school, community, vocation, recreation, and all other related areas. A wise selection of curriculum materials will include a well-balanced program appropriate to different maturity levels.

Teachers will be more effective if they know how to use supplementary helps. Under wise teacher-guidance, students will gain new information and experience through messages, discussions, and interviews; the study of maps, graphs, tables, globes; the reading of books, magazines, pamphlets; and the use of mass media.

SELECTION OF CURRICULUM MATERIALS

Someone in each Sunday school must be responsible for deciding what curriculum materials are to be used. The church must be sure that its curriculum is sound and effective and that the materials are in accord with its educational principles and policies. Denominational affiliation, the local church situation, particular needs of the community, and other factors may influence the decision.

The board of Christian education is the logical group to select curriculum materials. In some cases, the pastor or Sunday school superintendent makes the decision. Sometimes it is done by the departmental superintendent and his teachers.

When selecting curriculum materials, keep in mind the wisdom of using a theologically unified, correlated program throughout all age levels of the Sunday school. To achieve this objective, all classes might have to use materials produced by the same publisher. When the same curriculum is used in all age levels, broader Bible coverage results, duplication of lessons is avoided, and family discussion of Sunday school themes is encouraged.

The following criteria will assist the person, committee, board, or group, authorized to select curriculum materials.

Criteria Related to Lesson Content

Is material adapted to the age, experience, and needs of students?

Are the theological emphases in accord with your denomination or local church doctrinal statement?

Is extra-biblical material of high quality?

Are materials properly graded as to content and presentation?

Does it emphasize the total growth of the students?

Will it lead to Christian experience, maturity, and practice?

Does it correlate with the church's overall program of Christian education?

Does it stimulate church attendance and acceptance of responsibility?

Literary and Mechanical Features

Are the materials attractive and are the illustrations vivid?

Are the materials durably bound and of good quality?

Is vocabulary adapted to the age of the student?

Do stories capture attention?

Is subject matter clearly written?

Educational Helps for the Student
The Overall scope of the Student Book

Does each student have his own book?

Are there definite study aids and work assignments?

Does it provide for learning aids, such as illustrations, maps, pictures, records, or tapes?

Is it related to the students' experiences and maturity?

Does it encourage the student to discover answers on his own?

Individual Lessons or Units

Is there an interesting and gripping presentation, with good point of contact?

Are Bible portions identified easily?

Does it encourage active Bible study?

Is the lesson aim clearly defined?

Is material teachable, readable, and understandable?

Are lessons related to previous and subsequent studies?

Is handwork specifically related to content and student interests?

Are the activities used student-centered?

Is there proper progression?

Helps for the Teacher
The overall approach

Is there a plan or an outline for lesson preparation?

Does it list home assignments and projects?

Are there methods for applying the lesson to life situations?
Is there a bibliography of additional resources?
Are there learning aid suggestions such as maps, flannelgraph, charts, tables, murals, posters, recordings, slides, models?
Are there suggestions for involving the student in story writing, reports, role plays, pantomime, and projects?
Are there helps for bulletin boards, displays, illustrations?

Special emphases

Are seasonal days celebrated?
Are good citizenship and community responsibility stressed?
Are honesty, ethics, and good morals part of each lesson?
Do lessons provide a challenge to "full-time Christian service?"

CURRICULUM DESIGN

What lies behind the quarterlies used in Sunday school? Thousands of Sunday schools will distribute new materials at the beginning of the next quarter. Hundreds of thousands of students and their teachers will use these quarterlies as study guides. The printed page will make its impact on Sunday schools around the world. But few Sunday school leaders and teachers have ever analyzed the philosophies and policies that underlie these curriculum materials.

The Comparative Curriculum Chart supplies information about various types of curriculums. Based on questionnaires sent to several denominational and independent publishing houses, it presents a broad view of three different types of curriculum—Uniform, Departmentally Graded, and Closely Graded. The chart is only a guide. It is not intended to suggest which type of curriculum should be chosen. A study of the chart will assist in evaluating the methods and contents of all types. It will help to relate them to the educational principles and policies of a local church. (See chart pages 78 and 79.)

CURRICULUM ADAPTATION

Since adults will make up the largest part of the population in the future, special attention must be given to Christian education of people in this age group. Courses designed for men and women should relate the Scriptures to the specific problems of adult life and current social issues. Some speciality areas to keep in mind when designing a full-purpose curriculum might be leadership training, Bible study, and various elective subjects.

LEADERSHIP TRAINING

Leadership training is ideal for part of an adult program. E.T.T.A. training materials will strengthen the present leadership and challenge prospective teachers. A better understanding of the Bible and a new appreciation of the value of teaching methods will result. Every adult should be trained to study the Bible for himself and to present its message to others. He should know how to challenge students, how to understand them, and what to expect from them. Adults thus inspired and trained will be equipped to serve effectively in the total church program.

BIBLE STUDY COURSES

Though every effort should be made to encourage adults to take an active part in Sunday school, some men and women will be interested only to the extent of attending an adult class. The objective of the Sunday school should be to acquaint adults with the entire Bible. A rambling, almost aimless verse-by-verse commentary will never provide a broad familiarity with the whole Bible or any real application to contemporary life. However, a long-range curriculum of Bible study extending over a period of years will accomplish these results.

ELECTIVE COURSES

Interest is developing rapidly in elective courses, usually extending three months each for use in the senior high school, college and career, and adult departments. The use of elective courses among the youth will depend largely upon the leadership ability of the teachers, superintendents of these departments, and upon the specific needs of the students. Presently, several publishing houses produce excellent material for use on the elective basis designed specifically for a quarter's work. Topics include doctrine, personal evangelism, church history, non-Christian religions, leadership development, the Bible and science, Christian ethics, and a wide variety of other practical subjects. Such courses provide excellent teaching situations because students enroll on the basis of personal interest. These courses also serve as a stimulus for teachers in that they are able to teach courses of special interest.

COMPARATIVE CURRICULUM CHART

	UNIFORM	DEPARTMENTALLY GRADED	CLOSELY GRADED
Definition	A course of study using the same Sunday school lesson for all students.	A course of study arranged so that all students within the same department study the same Sunday school lesson.	A course of Sunday school lessons for use with students who are graded by one age or one public school grade.
Number of lessons taught each week	One lesson is provided for the entire Sunday school, usually graded by departments.	One lesson is provided for each department.	One lesson is provided for each school grade or age level.
Departments	Cradle Roll, Nursery, Kindergarten, Primary, Junior, Junior High, Senior High, College and Career, Adult		
Teaching staff required	One regular teacher required for each class. In some age groups, associate teachers and helpers may be of regular assistance.		
Assistant (substitute) teachers required	Prepared assistants teach in any department, adapting content and method to age level.	Prepared assistants may teach in any class within a given department.	Essential to have at least one assistant teacher for each grade.
Number of years in each cycle of lessons	The cycle ranges from five to eight years, depending on the curriculum planning committee.	The cycle varies with curriculums, usually the same as the number of years included in the department.	One year cycle of lessons is used for each school grade or age level.
Special emphases	Depending on policy of the publisher, evangelism, missions, family life, temperance, stewardship generally are included. Dated lessons may stress seasonal emphases such as Christmas, Easter, Mother's Day, patriotic holidays. Undated lessons include auxiliary seasonal and holiday themes. Many courses are available for worthwhile elective studies.		
Bible coverage	Approximately 35% to 50% of the Bible is included in each complete cycle and repeated in the next cycle.	A higher percentage of Bible usually covered. Some portions are repeated with a different emphasis, depending on age and characteristics of students.	

Teaching aids	Research materials include annual commentaries, teacher's weeklies, monthlies, and quarterlies.	The teacher's manual usually includes teaching aids and ideas, Bible study helps, background material, illustrations, suggestions for activities.	
Correlation of worship and class session	If worship periods are geared to any one age level, participation by others may be reduced.	Worship period is generally correlated with lesson theme and class session by departments.	Correlation of worship period and lesson theme is possible within each grade.
Aims and objectives	The Curriculum should implement the Sunday school's total educational program by providing a course of study to help the students to learn, understand, believe, and practice the message of the Bible.		
Extra-biblical materials	Editors and publishers usually provide illustrative and explanatory material to help both teachers and students. These include geography, history, archaeology, science, customs, current events.		
Major educational principles	One lesson adapted to the comprehension and understanding of each age group.	Lessons are graded by departments, combining 2 or 3 ages or school grades, gearing each to the understanding and experience of students.	Grading is by age or school grade, based on year to year change of needs, capacities, and abilities.
Learning Aids	Lesson helps suggest a wide variety of projected and non-projected visual aids, and audio aids. They are usually correlated with the lesson. Additional materials may be adapted.		
Student's study helps	Students' manuals, workbooks, and take-home papers are basic. Additional aids include handcraft, Bible puzzles, questions, home study manuals, projects, and other expressional activities. May also provide examinations, tests, and other measurements of progress.		

SUMMARY

Next to the teachers themselves, the curriculum is the most important factor affecting classroom learning. Hence, the choice of curriculum materials is very important.

When choosing curriculum for a Sunday school, be sure that its philosophy is compatible with your denominational doctrine, your church's constituency, and the ability of your teaching staff.

With the rising adult population, Sunday schools should consider providing maximum ministry to this expanding age group. Most contemporary Sunday schools are providing an elective program for their adults. Classes that might be offered in this type program include: leadership training, in-depth Bible study, personal evangelism, doctrinal studies, church history, Christian ethics, and other practical subjects.

REVIEW AND DISCUSSION QUESTIONS

1. Define the term *curriculum.*
2. Distinguish between *curriculum* and *curriculum materials* as used in this chapter.
3. What is the function of the curriculum?
4. What is the function of curriculum materials?
5. What person(s) should select curriculum and curriculum materials?
6. In evaluating curriculum materials, what basic criteria should be considered?
7. What educational helps for the students should be included in good curriculum materials?
8. List the three well-known types of curriculum.
9. What comprises a good adult curriculum?
10. Why is it wise to use the same publisher's curriculum materials throughout all departments of the Sunday school?

APPLICATION ACTIVITIES

1. Make a survey of the curriculum materials now in use in your Sunday school. Use the Comparative Curriculum Chart on pages 78 and 79.
2. Browse through a number of books dealing with curriculum structures to become thoroughly acquainted with various curriculum patterns.
3. Order sample curriculum materials from various publishers. Evaluate these on the basis of the curriculum chart and class findings.

RESOURCES

Colson, Howard P. and Rigdon, Raymond M. *Understanding Your Church's Curriculum.* Nashville: Broadman Press, 1981.

LeBar, Lois E. *Education That Is Christian.* Old Tappan, NJ: Fleming H. Revell Company, 1981. (Chapters 6-8)

MAJOR CURRICULUM PUBLISHERS

Many denominations publish or imprint their own curriculum and each reader is encouraged to investigate and become thoroughly familiar with all denominational materials. However, several inter-denominational publishing houses service thousands of churches with different types of evangelical curriculum for Sunday school. The addresses of six of them appear below.

Accent—B/P Publications
P.O. Box 15337
Denver, CO 80215

David C. Cook Publishing Company
850 North Grove Avenue
Elgin, IL 60120

Gospel Light Publishing Company
2300 Knoll Avenue
Ventura, CA 93006

Scripture Press Publications Inc.
1825 College Avenue
Wheaton, IL 60187

Standard Publishing Company
8121 Hamilton Avenue
Cincinnati, OH 45231

Union Gospel Press
P.O. Box 6059
Cleveland, OH 44101

Keeping on Target

11

Scripture provides us with an operational target at which to aim in Sunday school ministry. It helps to identify standards, it reminds us that record keeping is important, and it provides a guideline for evaluation.

STANDARDS

Just as an architect needs a blueprint, each Sunday school needs a standard for doing its task successfully. There must be objectives as well as plans for attaining them. The following simplified, yet comprehensive standard can be applied to every Sunday school regardless of denomination, size, or local situation. A Sunday school with limited equipment and simple organization can strive toward reaching this standard. Large schools with complex organizational structures are challenged by it.

Train every teacher
Offer a graded, biblical curriculum
Reach the entire Sunday school constituency
Lead students to Christ as Savior
Provide for maturity in Christ

TRAIN EVERY TEACHER

Teaching is important. God's Son was a teacher. When Jesus chose twelve to be with him that they might become teachers, he put his approval on the teacher's task. For three years those disciples were trained and finally they were commissioned to "Go teach."

Christ's command to teach is still valid. And preparation for teaching is still necessary to fulfill Christ's command in the church today. Therefore, do not criticize men and women who feel incompetent to teach a Sunday school class. If they are incompetent, the church is to blame for not preparing them to teach. If teachers catch a vision of the importance of teaching, they will accept the challenge and make the sacrifice to become better prepared for their great task.

OFFER A GRADED, BIBLICAL CURRICULUM

Life consists of stages of growth and development through which a child grows to youth and adulthood. As he passes through various stages of growth, he requires different foods, clothing, exercise, care, sleep, and understanding. Wise parents plan for these changing and growing needs of their children.

Public school educators pattern their whole program on the basis of this graded principle. Thus, students progress from kindergarten to eighth grade—and then high school and college.

Christian educators have accepted the graded principle in order to provide a comprehensive and more complete knowledge of the Bible. Since it is the primary source of truth about God, about man, and about the world, the Bible should be covered at least as thoroughly and systematically in the Sunday school as secular subjects are covered in the public school.

REACH YOUR ENTIRE SUNDAY SCHOOL CONSTITUENCY

Any country is vitally affected by the availability of the Bible to its people. Some churches are not aware of the value of the teaching ministry of the Sunday school. Others are content to minister to the people of their own church group. Consequently, only a fragmentary effort is exerted to teach the vast army of boys, girls, and grown-ups who face eternity without a knowledge of Christ.

Every Sunday school leader must recognize that the Sunday school is reaching only one person of a possible four or five. If a Sunday school has a present enrollment of 400, there are between 1,200 and 1,600 unreached students for which the school is responsible. What responsibility! "Blow the trumpet and warn the people. . . But if the watchman see the sword come, and blow not the trumpet, and the people be not warned. . . his blood will I require at the watchman's hand" (Ezek. 33:3,6).

LEAD STUDENTS TO CHRIST AS SAVIOR

A large majority of all conversions take place before a person reaches twenty years of age. More people are converted at sixteen than at twenty-six. Fewer people join the church after they are twenty-one. Statistics also reveal the startling fact that many adult converts lose their interest within five years. Of the children brought up and led to Christ in the Sunday school, the majority continue to grow in the Lord.

If the church accepts its God-given task of evangelism—winning the lost to Christ—it becomes the business of the church to provide and prepare evangelists. Every Sunday school teacher is a potential evangelist with opportunity and responsibility for leading his or her students to Jesus Christ.

PROVIDE FOR MATURITY IN CHRIST

No Sunday school should be satisfied until its administrative personnel and teachers are concerned about the growth in grace of those who are already saved. Those who have accepted Christ need to be guided into full Christian maturity. Bible study and prayer; worship and witnessing; surrender and service; going and giving; training and teaching—all these should be included in the well-rounded, down-to-earth, practical experience of a growing, maturing child of God.

RECORDS

The church is both organism and organization. As an organism it is the body of Christ made up of believers who depend on their pastors and teachers to provide spiritual feeding and growth. As an organization it expects efficiency, evaluation, and other such activities which accurate records supply.

THE SIX-POINT RECORD SYSTEM

The Six-Point System has been favorably accepted as a standard in many Sunday schools. The system is built on the theory that students can be stimulated to be present and on time at every session, to share in the offering, to prepare their lessons, and to bring their Bibles. These requirements are easily within reach of every Sunday school student.

Attendance and preparation of the lesson are awarded the same point value because they largely determine the scholastic progress of the student. In recognition of the vital relationship between church and Sunday school, the student is graded on attendance at one service of worship at least. A scale of the relative importance of each requirement is suggested. The points may be multipled by 100 or 1,000:

Attendance 3
Punctuality 1
Bible 1

Offering 1
Church attendance 1
Lesson preparation and class participation 3

Many Sunday schools use the Six-Point Record System in all departments. Other use a modification of four points for the Kindergarten and Primary children. When four points are used, they might include:

Attendance 7
Punctuality 1
Offering 1
Memory verse or Bible 1

Further adaptations can be made to this system to meet other departmental needs.

ESSENTIAL MATERIALS FOR KEEPING RECORDS

Many different forms accomplish this work. It is advisable to examine various records systems for comparative values and adaptability to your program. Particular attention should be given to the enrollment record card, individual record envelope, departmental record card, and monthly report card. These records indicate something of the student's spiritual condition and help build character habits.

Efficiency in marking and storing records is vital if they are to be useful. A well-trained general secretary is essential. It is his responsibility to assist in training departmental and class secretaries so that accurate and meaningful records are consistently kept and turned in to a central office or file.

FOLLOW-UP OF ABSENTEES

Trained teachers, a well-structured curriculum, and a plan for recognizing progress should provide genuine incentive for regular attendance. As a further guarantee against students dropping out, there should be a suitable, workable plan for absentee follow-up. Each Sunday school needs its own plan, but here is a generally accepted pattern which uses other leaders of the Sunday school and strengthens the impact of the church's concern.

First Sunday, Student Notified

All absences are carefully recorded by the secretary. It is his job to notify the teacher whose duty it is to contact the student. Sending a postal card to the absentee may be all that is necessary the first week.

Second Sunday, Teacher calls.

The secretary notifies the teacher that a student has been absent for two Sundays, and the teacher makes a personal visit. Some teachers have their own personal notebook or chart so that they can keep close contact with their students. They realize the value of personal interest and follow through on absentees without a reminder from the secretary.

Third Sunday, Departmental Superintendent Calls

The teacher's visit should be followed by a visit from the departmental superintendent. The secretary must provide the departmental superintendent with the names and addresses of all students who have been absent three consecutive Sundays.

Fourth Sunday, Superintendent Is Notified

The general superintendent may be most effective in bringing back a delinquent student. In case of illness, it is equally important that he be notified. When the absentee is a member of the church, the pastor, as well as the superintendent, should be contacted. The superintendent and/or the pastor should then decide what should be done about each individual case. It would be a good policy for the secretary to notify both the pastor and superintendent when any student is ill, or absent because of other emergencies.

In every class, members should have a genuine interest in the other members of the class. This will result naturally in class efforts at contacting absentees which may be either organized or spontaneous. The teacher should foster mutual concern.

All Sunday schools have students who are unable to be present because of sickness, the need to care for others, or other conditions over which they have no control. Where a student cannot attend, the teacher should make special arrangements to help the student keep up with class progress. Inviting parental cooperation also strengthens the church-home ties. In cases of extended illness or other excused absences, there should be adequate contact so the student will feel that he belongs.

EVALUATION

Both measuring and evaluating are vital to the success of a Sunday school. Evaluation includes appraising or judging the worth of a situation, program, or a planned experience. It means investigation into "how much" or "how well." Measuring deals generally with skills and knowledge, is periodical, and considers external things. Considering these areas, attention must be paid to the initial objectives of Christian education and the ultimate or immediate goals set forth in the school's program.

EVALUATING THE SCHOOL

Evaluation of the total Sunday school implies careful scrutiny of attendance and enrollment records. It also includes inventories of finances and equipment. Teacher-student ratios and curriculum are measured against established aims of the total program or particular areas. This becomes a vital aspect of growth since results of evaluation will give direction to further scheduling, purchasing, and training. It will indicate errors and channel corrective means as well as give direction for improvement.

Christian education results in change. Evaluation of the organization, its leadership, program, and curriculum, including facilities and equipment, will indicate the amount, direction, and rate of change.

EVALUATING THE CLASSROOM

The classroom, teacher, and students are the grassroots of Christian education and the heart of the Sunday school. The most effective evaluation can be carried on at this level. This evaluation includes an objective study of the progress of the student, the teaching process, and the teacher.

The Student

Student growth is essential to Christian education and can be measured and evaluated in terms of knowledge, attitudes, values, and ultimately in conduct. Testing in the area of acquired knowledge is the easiest and most frequently used. This involves the use of true-false, matching, completion, and multiple-choice tests based on the biblical material currently being studied.

Attitudes and values are not easily measured and progress is difficult to evaluate. These involve insight into the student and the changes in convictions as a result of the materials taught. Diagrams, checklists or choices, and rating scales can be used to indicate student attitudes on ethical questions.

Evaluating progress in terms of conduct is the most sure but the most time-consuming for it demands observation and understanding of each student in and out of class. This can be done in terms of the classroom experience on the basis of self-rating scales, sociodrama and role-playing where behavioral reaction to problem situations can be studied and evaluated. Checklists and questionnaires are helpful but take considerable time and thought in their preparation.

The Teaching Process

Observation of the teaching staff in terms of improvement and evaluating effectiveness at a given point is contingent upon the methods used. Appropriateness of teaching techniques must be continually evaluated. Presentation of material and student reaction and participation serve as a basis for this.

The Teacher As Leader

Evaluation of the teacher as leader comes about in terms of progress in spiritual growth, performance of those tasks assigned, and demonstration of Christian character. It involves the development of individual leadership, personality, and the ability to function in the particular place of service effectively. This can be done by the use of rating sheets and self-rating scales, check charts, and self appraisal.

Evaluation generally leads to recognition of work well done. The use of honor and recognition certificates for students and leaders is desirable.

SUMMARY

Standards, records, and evaluation are three proven instruments for helping organizations become more effective and grow.

Important standards for all Sunday schools to set up and attain are: train every teacher; offer a graded, biblical curriculum; reach its entire constituency; lead students to Christ; and provide for maturing in Christ.

Well-kept records are a key to success in Sunday schools. Many schools find the Six-Point Record System to be effective. This method assigns point values to these six areas: attendance, punctuality, bringing Bible, offering, church attendance, and lesson preparation and participation. Of course modification of these areas must take place in some departments, but this system can provide the motivation many schools need to get on the track to effectiveness.

Follow-up of absentees is also a necessary procedure to keep students active. A good plan for following up student absentees is: first Sunday—secretary notifies teacher; second Sunday—teacher calls; third Sunday—departmental superintendent calls; fourth Sunday—general superintendent notified.

Evaluation provides a measure for determining "how well" and "how much" your school is attaining its standards.

Evaluating the school will indicate what changes or corrections are needed in the program.

Student evaluation indicates progress. Student factual knowledge is the easiest to determine by testing. Measurement of student attitudes and values is harder but can be handled with the use of diagrams, checklists, choices, or rating scales. Evaluating student conduct is the hardest because it involves much time on the part of the evaluator both in and out of class.

If evaluating of the teacher and the teaching process is done appropriately, many positive benefits can result. Among these are: more effective teacher-student communication; better presentation of material; and a high degree of student participation.

REVIEW AND DISCUSSION QUESTIONS
1. What are the practical values of using a Sunday school standard?
2. List the points of a basic standard which are applicable to every Sunday school.
3. How did Jesus illustrate the importance of teaching?
4. Why is it imperative to train the teaching staff?
5. Why is a graded, biblical curriculum necessary?
6. What is the responsibility of the Sunday school in evangelistic efforts?
7. Give three illustrations that prove the value of well-kept records.
8. Describe the Six-Point Record System.
9. Who is responsible for keeping attendance records?
10. Describe the plan for organized follow-up over a monthly period.
11. Why should the Sunday school be evaluated?
12. Discuss various ways to evaluate the student, the teaching process, the teacher.

APPLICATION ACTIVITIES
1. Choose one phase of the Sunday school ministry to develop a plan of standardization. You may want to compare your denomination's plan with that of other denominations and publishers.
2. If you have access to a Christian college or Bible school, consider auditing a few Christian education classes or consulting with one or more of the faculty about special needs and problems of your own Sunday school.

3. Contact your Sunday school secretary for information on the record system used in your Sunday school. Is the system adequate? What purpose does it serve? How can it be strengthened?

4. Suggest some measurement procedures or checklists to evaluate your present Sunday school program. Then make a list of improvements you believe your school should make. Prayerfully share these observations with the proper authorities.

RESOURCES

Byrne, H. W. *Improving Church Education.* Birmingham, AL: Religious Education Press, 1979. (Chapters 4 and 5 deal with the subject of evaluation in detail.)

Edge, Findley B. *Teaching For Results.* Nashville: Broadman Press, 1956.

Towns, Elmer. *The Successful Sunday School and Teachers Guidebook.* Carol Stream, IL: Creation House, 1979. (Chapter 52)

Patterns for the Future

12

The preceding chapters have described the history and current status of Sunday school. It has had an exciting and effective ministry of bringing men, women, boys, and girls into a saving knowledge of Jesus Christ, enriching their Christian lives, and preparing them to serve Christ. Sunday school has been used of God in the past and is being used effectively today.

But Sunday school cannot expect to stay in the forefront of Christian education by resting on the accomplishments of the past. It must keep a forward-looking profile if it is to keep up with the changing educational scene.

Sunday schools should evaluate, therefore, their current programs to determine those elements that are advancing them toward predetermined goals and those that could be changed in favor of more up-to-date techniques and activities.

Both outside influences and developing emphases must be considered as the Sunday school plans for the future. Current strengths need to be preserved and future trends understood. A number of current conditions will have a direct impact upon the Sunday school of the future.

OUTSIDE INFLUENCES

Changes outside the Sunday school strongly affect its ministry. Sunday schools meeting changing needs have always had the strongest impact. The Sunday school of the future must respond to the following developments if it is to continue to have its influence.

INCREASE IN CHRISTIAN SCHOOLS

For several reasons, more and more families in the past two decades have found the education offered in public schools to be inadequate. Many Christian families that can afford an alternative school have banded together either in a community or a church and worked to establish Christian day schools. These schools teach from a biblical perspective and their curriculum includes study of the Bible. Most students attend these schools along with Sunday school and this has created new challenges. Christian day school students are generally more proficient in Bible knowledge than students attending public schools, thus creating a potential imbalance. As more children in a church attend Christian day schools, however, the problem of uneven Bible knowledge might be alleviated. In these schools the curriculum of the day school and the Sunday school should be coordinated to provide complementary Bible study and to avoid duplication of lessons.

In Sunday schools where only a few of the children are attending Christian day schools, enrichment experiences could be provided for the Christian day school students. Perhaps some of the Christian day school students could be used as teaching assistants in classes of younger age students. Intergenerational grouping could also help alleviate this problem.

INCREASED ADULT POPULATION

Sunday schools must develop a new emphasis on adults and a new image as an adult ministry. Statistical surveys indicate a steady increase in the proportionate adult population. Most churches are also experiencing an increase in the number of adults attending Sunday school.

Many Sunday schools have arranged to accommodate larger groups of adults and have begun to project their programs to minister to these groups. This has required a change in classroom techniques, lesson content, and organizational methodology. With larger adult groups, the range of interests also multiplies. All these interests will not be served in one large class for adults. Sunday schools will need to plan smaller group studies. These studies will be on an elective basis and might include studies of a book of the Bible, a current Christian book, or problem area in Christian living. Groupings might also be arranged to develop the interests of adults in a particular age group.

INCREASED INTEREST IN SPIRITUAL GROWTH

People in general have a renewed interest in spiritual things. More and more self-help books are being published and many study courses have been developed. Even secular publications include articles about people who claim to have had spiritual experiences.

The Sunday school should capitalize on this new spiritual awareness. The desire for spiritual growth needs to be cultivated.

It indicates a need to go beyond a basic knowledge of biblical facts to deeply meaningful life application lessons from the Bible. Christians will expect to be challenged by their Sunday school classes, not just informed.

INCREASED ACADEMIC INTEREST IN CHRISTIAN EDUCATION

Certainly the field of Christian education, and more specifically local church education, is much broader than the Sunday school. But what students are studying in Christian institutions at the undergraduate and graduate levels and what is happening in the local church are inseparable. On that basis, local church Christian education looks quite healthy. In fact, never before in the history of the church have more Christian education courses been taught by more professors in more schools. Thousands of students are majoring in Christian education, learning how to administer a variety of educational programs, not the least of which is the Sunday school.

Even seminaries which had previously downplayed Christian education are now insisting on a stronger educational training program for pastors and church leaders.

As the number of Christian leaders graduating from Christian institutions of higher learning increases, so also should the places for them to serve. Their impact should be significantly felt in all areas of Christian education and especially in the Sunday school. Wherever these graduates can help further a church's ministry, they should be employed and used. Even though the Sunday school is primarily a ministry carried out by laymen, professional input can profitably be used to better define and implement its goals.

DEVELOPING EMPHASES

The future is bright for Sunday school ministry with many new emphases on the horizon. Sunday schools planning for the future need to be aware of these emphases.

THE FAMILY

Christians today are becoming increasingly alarmed about the breakdown of the family. The sharp increases of the number of divorces in Christian families, childhood and teenage delinquency, and both parents working outside the home have brought about a demand for more emphasis on the family in the Sunday school.

93

It appears clear that the problems facing traditional family structures and lifestyles will not get better but will probably get worse. What a challenge for the Sunday school! This vital ministry must find ways to better meet the needs of families. Teachers should be in close touch with the homes of their students so they can better direct their teaching toward fulfilling their students' needs.

Another technique that might be used is *intergenerational learning.* This combines various ages in the same class so that students can benefit from the perspectives and experience of all age levels. If all family members participated in the same class, presented their views on the lesson content, and applied the biblical truths to their lives, better communication and sharing might result. If this type approach is adopted, a greater variety of materials incorporating intergenerational and family learning need to be produced.

BIBLE TEACHING

Sunday schools that teach the Bible and apply its truths to the lives of their students have been the most successful. Whenever the central focus of the Sunday school is diverted from the Bible, problems arise. Today those Sunday schools that stress the truths of God's Word are growing both in numbers and spirituality. When the Bible is faithfully taught and systematically applied to the students' lives, the Sunday school grows and becomes more effective. Campaigns and contests may increase attendance for a time, but long lasting results stem from offering biblical answers to present-day challenges.

As in the past and present, the Bible must be kept as the central theme and focus of the Sunday school's message. Even though methods for teaching it and the interests of the people studying it might change, the Bible must remain the only source of faith and practice.

NEW CURRICULUM RESOURCES

The quality of curriculum materials for use in the Sunday school has never been better. Denominational and independent publishing houses using the most up-to-date materials and methods are now producing attractive, creative, and useable materials for every level of the Sunday school. Along with the traditional guides and quarterlies, many multimedia resources are becoming available for use in Sunday school. Curriculum producers have proven that they have the expertise to develop and design effective educational materials. These products will be needed in the future for implementing programs for intergenerational learning, enrichment for Christian day school students, family-learning experiences, and spiritual growth studies.

LEADERSHIP TRAINING

Increasing numbers of church and Sunday school administrators have seen the benefits of training their teachers and leaders. This has resulted in greater numbers of materials and programs available for teacher and leadership training and more and more Sunday schools emphasizing and conducting teacher training programs.

The future challenges for leadership training are as far-reaching as the number of possibilities for Sunday school. As Sunday school ministries change, so also will leadership training. Where structures and roles of Sunday school classes change, more leaders and teachers with different skills and techniques will be needed.

SUMMARY

What will Sunday schools be like in the future? No one can really answer that question. Sunday school will be exactly what the Lord wills it to be with our help. The Lord has blessed and used the Sunday school in the past and is using it today. We can expect him to continue to bless it as it seeks to accomplish his commission to go into all the world and make disciples of all nations. With careful analysis of past experiences and insightful planning for the future, the Sunday school will continue to grow stronger and more effective as an instrument for winning people to Christ, nurturing them in the faith, and preparing them for future service.

REVIEW AND DISCUSSION QUESTIONS

1. Describe the process the Sunday school should use in planning for the future.
2. Why do you think the Sunday school faced problems when its central focus strayed away from the Bible?
3. Why has Sunday school attendance dropped in many mainline denominational churches?

4. What effect has the decline in quality of public school education had on the Sunday school?
5. How has the Sunday school adapted multimedia approaches to learning?
6. What accounts for the recent changes in the structure of Sunday school attendance?
7. How can the Sunday school better minister to families?
8. What can the Sunday school do to capitalize on the increased number of Christian education graduates?
9. Why is the increased adult population an asset rather than a liability for the Sunday school?
10. What changes in leadership training will have to be made to meet future Sunday school needs?

APPLICATION ACTIVITIES

1. Evaluate the flexibility of your own Sunday school. How many significant changes have you made in recent years? What areas might still benefit from change?
2. Write a letter this week to some organization responsible for helping your Sunday school succeed. It might be a denominational Christian education office or a publisher. Ask key questions regarding some of the problems you are presently facing.
3. Spend some time over the next few weeks designing a basic Bible test which can be administered to students who have spent several years in your Sunday school. Balance the questions between Old and New Testaments and gear the test to about the ninth or tenth grade level. Ask students throughout the Sunday school (or perhaps a random sample) to complete the test and indicate only their ages not their names. Evaluate the results and grade your Sunday school on the effectiveness of communicating Bible content.

RESOURCES

Lynn, Robert W. and Wright, Elliott. *The Big Little School*. Nashville: Abingdon Press, 1980.

Willis, Wesley R. *200 Years and Still Counting!* Wheaton, IL: Victor Books, 1979.